Images 32
The best of British contemporary illustration 2008

Images 32

Edited and published by
The Association of Illustrators
2nd Floor, Back Building
150 Curtain Road
London
EC2A 3AT

Tel. +44 (0)20 7613 4328
Fax +44 (0)20 7613 4417
info@theaoi.com
www.theAOI.com

ISBN 978-0-9558076-9-5
Production in China by
Hong Kong Graphics and Printing Ltd
Tel: (852) 2976 0289
Fax: (852) 2976 0292

The Association of Illustrators

AOI Volunteer Council of Management
Beach, Russell Cobb, Andrew Coningsby, Adam Graff,
Rod Hunt, Simon Pemberton

AOI Chair
Russell Cobb

AOI Deputy Chair
Rod Hunt

Company Secretary
Rod Hunt

AOI Images Committee
Silvia Baumgart (until Feb 08), Adam Graff, Rod Hunt, Bethany King,
Sian Rees (from Nov 07), Sabine Reimer, William Webb (until Oct 07)

Advisors
Stephanie Alexander, Alison Branagan, Ruth Gladwin,
Chris Haughton, Tony Healey, Matt Johnson, Christine Jopling,
Robert Lands, Alison Lang, Samantha Lewis, Simon Stern, Fig Taylor,
Anna Vernon, Bee Willey

Manager
Silvia Baumgart (until Feb 08)

Interim Manager
Derek Brazell (from Feb 08)
derek@theaoi.com

Images Co-ordinator
Sabine Reimer
images@theaoi.com

Marketing and Events Co-ordinator
Bethany King
events@theaoi.com

Publications/Senior Membership Co-ordinator
Derek Brazell
derek@theaoi.com

Membership Co-ordinators
Nicolette Hamilton and Jo Young (until April 08)
info@theaoi.com

Finance Officer
Ian Veacock BA(Hons) FCCA
finance@theaoi.com

Book Design
Simon Sharville
www.simonsharville.co.uk

Patrons:

Images 32
The best of British contemporary illustration 2008

Contents

About the **AOI**

The Association of Illustrators was established in 1973 to advance and protect illustrators' rights, and is a non-profit making trade association dedicated to its members' professional interests and the promotion of contemporary illustration. As the only body to represent illustrators and campaign for their rights in the UK, the AOI has successfully increased the standing of illustration as a profession and improved the commercial and ethical conditions of employment for illustrators. On behalf of its members and with their continued support, the AOI can achieve goals that would be difficult or impossible for creators to attempt alone.

A voice for illustration
The AOI provides a voice for professional illustrators and by weight of numbers and expertise is able to enforce the rights of freelance illustrators at every stage of their careers, enabling individual illustrators to deal with today's market. AOI liaises with national and international organisations, art buyers, agents and illustrators over industry problems and campaigns against unfair contracts and terms of trade.

Campaigning and Networking
The AOI is responsible for establishing the right for illustrators to retain ownership of their artwork and helped to establish the secondary rights arm of the Designers and Artists Copyright Society (DACS), the UK visual arts collecting society. In addition, it lobbies parliament for better legislation for illustrators though the Creators Rights Alliance (CRA) and the British Copyright Council (BCC). The AOI is also a founder member of the European Illustrators Forum (EIF) a network of 19 member associations in Europe established to exchange information, co-ordinate exhibitions and conferences and create a stronger force for illustrators within Europe and the European Commission.

Pro-Action: Illustration Campaign and Liaison Group
Pro-Action is a new committee established by the Association of Illustrators and the Society of Artists Agents to deal with the problems facing illustrators in today's market place. It's aims is to tackle fee erosion, increasingly detrimental contract terms from clients, and issues that may arise between illustrators and their representatives. These factors have increasingly become a negative force effecting creators of visual material working in the commercial communications arena over the last 25 years. For further information please visit www.pro-action.org.uk.

Information and Support Services
In the past year, the AOI has continued to improve services to its members. Members of the AOI not only sustain campaigning and networking to improve working conditions for all, they benefit personally from AOI services.

Members stay informed with our wide range of events and seminars. Varoom magazine, UP info poster and the monthly Despatch newsletter keep members up to date with events, practice and developments in the industry. Members receive up to 50% off our topical range of events and forums, themes ranging from children's books, to self-promotion, business planning and up-to-the-minute industry debates.

Resources to help illustrators succeed
Members receive large discounts on essential publications, including the Images annual, The Illustrator's Guide to Law and Business Practice, Survive - The Illustrator's Guide to a Professional Career and our range of targeted directory listings of illustration commissioners. Members of the AOI receive discounts in art shops around the country.

Resources to help commissioners succeed
The AOI's Guide to Commissioning Illustration will save time and money by guiding commissioners safely through all pitfalls of the commissioning process. Commissioners receive Images, the only jury-selected source book in the UK, free of charge. Our online portfolios give commissioners looking for the perfect artist for their projects access to more than 8000 classified images and the creator's contact details in a click.

Essential professional and business advice
Members have access to a free dedicated hotline for legal, ethical and pricing advice, discounted consultations with our pool of industry specialists including business advisors, a life coach, chartered accountants and portfolio consultants.

Promotion
Members can receive substantial discounts on the AOI's online portfolios and our Images competition and exhibition, showcasing the best of British contemporary illustration. The annual is the only jury-selected source book, despatched to over 4000 prominent commissioners of illustration in the UK and overseas.

Inspiration
Talks with leading illustrators, industry debates and discounted entry to competitions and exhibitions. Members receive a free subscription to Varoom, the journal of illustration and made images, a 90 page magazine the UK's creative industry has been waiting for. Varoom is a sumptuous celebration of 'made' images. It features interviews with leading illustrators and image-makers as well as in-depth articles on different aspects and themes of contemporary illustration. It's stimulating line-up of interviews, profiles, history and polemic make Varoom essential reading for everyone interested in visual communication.

Contact
To request further information or a membership application form please telephone +44 (0)20 7613 4328 or email info@theaoi.com

Website
Visit the AOI's website at **www.theAOI.com** for details of the Association's activities, forthcoming events, online tickets, history of the AOI, and to order publications or view online portfolios.

Welcome to Images 2008.
Could it be our best year ever?

In almost every awards book, whoever writes the introduction usually says that it wasn't a vintage year. 'Mmm, there were some good things, maybe one or two really good things, but… not a vintage year'.

Well, at the risk of going against the grain (or worse still, sounding like an old softie) I'm going to state right here and now that this IS definitely a vintage year.

Innovative and eclectic, Images 2008 reveals the sea change that's been happening in illustration over the past few years. Ad agencies and editors have had their budgets trimmed, and as technology's leapt forward, illustration increasingly appears, to those who commission it, as an affordable way to get startling and original imagery.

Images 2008 brilliantly reflects that upsurge, with a book full of innovative, eclectic, sometimes visionary work, representing all that's best in current British illustration.

And like the work inside it, the book itself is moving with the times. Our new format is just one of many exciting changes to Images, and there are more to come – so watch this space.

The Images awards night and supporting exhibition have grown steadily in popularity, and our touring show is spreading the gospel across the UK and overseas.

Images has always been more than just a tool for commissioning work. It remains the only jury selected awards book that also celebrates and rewards excellence in British illustration, and as such there's no better stimulant for artists and illustrators.

There's never been healthier competition in illustration. Never been more opportunities for the best work. And I'm not sure any previous Images has better reflected the fantastic talent in British illustration.

Congratulations to all this year's selected artists and winners. And a massive thank-you to every single person who had the bravery and vision to commission work as exciting as this.

Not a vintage year? Well, all I can say is: beat that, 2009.

Russell Cobb,
AOI Chairman

Introduction by **David Downton**

Over the last decade David Downton has established a reputation as one of Europe's leading fashion illustrators. His work appears regularly in magazines, advertising campaigns, books and gallery shows. Alongside his commercial work he has produced portraits of fashion icons such as Erin O' Connor, Dita Von Teese and Catherine Deneuve. Last year he launched a magazine, Pour Quoi Pas?, dedicated to fashion illustration.

"Keep Calm and Carry on" advised a popular World War II slogan and once again it is everywhere; on T-shirts and bags, on post cards and posters (and t-towels and mouse mats for all I know). Obviously, it says something about our troubled environmental, financial and geopolitical times and, like Penguin deckchairs and Pantone mugs, (seriously, wouldn't you prefer to buy Pantone paper than mugs?) it appeals to the design nostalgics amongst us.

For illustrators too, it is a slogan with particular resonance. As Adrian Shaughnessy so adeptly pointed out in last year's introduction, our industry is facing unpredictable times. When I was asked to write about the current state of illustration for this annual, I realised how little I know about what is going on 'out there'. The reasons, or at least my excuses, are twofold; Firstly, I have always worked on my own in my studio, mostly to the rhythm of Radio 4 (my knowledge of many other subjects, financial, medical, and horticultural is, therefore, pretty impressive; broad rather than deep). Working in what might romantically be called 'isolation', can be a distorting mirror. It is quite possible (and sometimes comforting) to believe you are the only illustrator. In the 80s and 90s, I used to advertise in Contact, and I dreaded its arrival; the sheer heft of it! All these people are Illustrators? Secondly, for the last 10 years or more I have been working principally as a fashion illustrator, a discipline with its own codes and hierarchies that seem strangely unrelated to mainstream illustration.

I became an illustrator because I was 'good at drawing'. I was better than my friends. I was the best at school. I always got the Art Prize anyway. My foundation course therefore came as something of a blow. Everyone was good at drawing! I spent 4 years at Art College sulking because I wasn't special anymore. Still, it was obvious I was not cut out to be a fine artist; they were dark and dangerous and kept their coats on at parties. Graphics/Illustration students on the other hand seemed to be channelling Marcel Marceau in their braces and stripy t-shirts and brightly coloured kickers (I include YOU Trevor Beattie). I limped out of college with a bad degree and no confidence (seeing my meretricious copies of Glynn Boyd Harte, a visiting lecturer announced that he could "see nothing of any value" in my entire portfolio.)

I took a job with a market research company in London, and it was only when mind-numbing boredom forced me to do something after a year, that I took what was left of my portfolio to the offices of a teenage magazine next door. Astonishingly, they gave me a job. That was in the early 80s. I worked for the next dozen years. Taking on anything that came up. "Wagging my tail when the phone rang" in Chris Burke's immortal phrase. These were the years of Red Star, of jobs falling like ripe fruit, when art directors were Gods (not kids). It was a pre computer and pre picture library world. And, with no email, there was always a deadline dodging excuse. They were heady days. One well-known illustrator of my acquaintance would, on occasion, call a courier to pick-up artwork and then start it. I worked pretty much without direction; Maps and menus and kids books and OUP and CUP, and on one memorable occasion a sex manual. By 1996, I was successful (nice house, two children, ringing phone) and once more bored to tears. "It's like being a hamster in a wheel", said a friend of mine "it's only worse when they take the wheel".

Then, a phone call changed everything. A commission to go to Paris, and draw at the couture shows.

I had received occasional fashion commissions, but did not consider myself a fashion illustrator. (For one thing they had exotic names like Zoltan, Antonio and Viramontes). But I did know and love the work of Gruau, Eric, Bouché and Bérard – masters in their field. To me they were artists; artists who's subject was fashion. And personally, I have always felt that fashion is as legitimate a subject for art as any other. What I loved was the fluidity of their drawing, the reductive line underscored by peerless draughtsmanship. 'Telling the story of the dress' was how one fashion illustrator put it, but it was more; it told the story around the dress. The time, the place and the woman.

Entering the fashion world was another awakening. You were more likely to be working with a fashion editor or designer, than an art editor; you went to shows and (gulp) parties. Initially, I saw all this as going behind enemy lines. Gradually I came to view it as my pass into the Kingdom of Indulgence. Fashion, lets face it, is an easy target. It has its share of air-headed, ambitious egomaniacs. But no more than its share. Certainly no more than you find in the theatre, film or fine art worlds. Abfab is one perspective. But there is another. At its best (and couture is its best) it is a magic lantern show, suffused with drama and passion and a reckless creativity. Unconvinced? Then take a look at the 'so wrong it's right' magic of Christian Lacroix's colour palette. Or find your patience rewarded (you might wait two hours) at Galliano/Dior show of such dazzling complexity and dark beauty that it leaves you breathless.

So, let's get to the point – how do things look in 2008? I would say that there has never been a better, or more confusing, time to be a (fashion) illustrator. Today there is no hegemony, no prescribed style of working. Fashion illustration encompasses Julie Verhoven's sexy, scrawled in the margins stream of consciousness and Jason Brooks' perfect-world club culture imagery. It ranges from François Berthoud's haunting monotypes and linocuts to Mats Gustafsson's floating, dream like figures. The tensions between hand drawn and digital imagery have long since disappeared and at the top of the profession everyone has their own, distinct, handwriting.

The market for fashion illustration certainly keeps shifting. The high-end glossies no longer use drawing (I do not count the 'handbag and horoscope' commissions, which are little more than useful devices for plugging holes left by copy), nor have they, consistently, for decades. It is their loss. But a door slams and a window opens. Today it is the ever proliferating, and increasingly lavish, niche publications that regularly commission some of the most innovative illustration. I will leave the cynics amongst you to make the link between size zero budgets and the relative costs of an illustrator and a photographer (and his or her model, hairdresser, makeup artist, stylist and assorted assistants...) Advertising seldom uses fashion illustration; it is apparently not sexy enough. And sex, as we all know, sells. But again, new markets emerge; Illustrators are increasingly collaborating with fashion designers on printed textiles, set design and brand imagery. There is also a surge in the number of collectors of original work, and a healthy upswing in the prices great pieces can achieve; a Gruau drawing recently sold in New York for $80 000. Elsewhere, fashion illustration can be seen, in one form or another, on ceramics, clubfliers, book and CD covers, even in animation. All of which indicates that the much-vaunted 'revival in interest' of a few years ago may, after all, be real.

And what of illustration generally? My suspicion is, that as long as there is a God in Heaven (I mean Ronald Searle in the South of France, obviously) and Sara Fanelli and David Hughes and (insert illustrator of your choice) are working at the top of their game, things will be just fine. Though this is not an advice column, and though calm may not be your current state of mind, I would suggest the best thing is to carry on.

Comment by Paul Belford, This is Real Art

Paul is a partner and creative director of This is Real Art, a creative company that ignores the traditional boundaries between advertising, digital and graphic design.
Previously he was a creative director at AMV BBDO, the UK's largest advertising agency.
He has more D&AD Pencils for art direction than any other art director in the world.

There's never been a better time to be an illustrator. Especially if you're an art director, graphic designer, artist, photographer or retoucher.

Scarcely a day goes by when I don't see some interesting digital illustration created by a person who isn't actually a professional illustrator. Hurrah for Apple. Hurrah for Adobe. But hang on, haven't we always had the tools to create illustration - pencils, pens, paintbrushes, ink, paint, paper?

There seems to be something about the ubiquitous Apple Mac that frees us and encourages experimentation. The possibilities are infinite. The only limit is your imagination and all that.

This is, of course, great news for 'proper' illustrators. Because many of them have all this at their finger tips and they can actually draw. An increasingly valuable skill when the person doing the comissioning has exactly the same tools sitting on their desk as you do.

Commissions come in all shapes and sizes. But so long as the illustrator has the ability to bring something unique to the party in terms of ideas and craft skills, then business should be good.

And business has clearly been good for some this year. Two huge commercial campaigns have stood out for me (both, incdentally, by the same ad agency). The **Robinsons** and **Vodafone** posters have, in effect, been sponsored public art exhibitions along the streets of Britain. (48-sheet and 6-sheet posters are not an eyesore. What some idiots put on them is the eyesore.) These campaigns have brightened our journeys but also, I'm sure, shifted a few warehouses full of Robinsons kids drinks and a huge amount of Vodafone services. If you didn't know before that the internet was mobile or that Vodafone had free weekend call packages, you do now.

Hats off to **Adrian Johnson** for the beautiful Robinsons illustrations. These posters really are good enough to put on a wall. The illustration style is charming, distinctive and perfectly suited to the subject matter. I particularly like the way in which the type is integrated with the illustration style. This is an advantage that illustration often has over photography. One useful trick when designing layouts, is to reduce the number of elements on the page. So if something can magically transform an image and headline from two elements into one, then I'm more than interested.

The fish4 newspaper campaign using the wonderfully quirky illustrations and handlettering of Andy Smith also employs this tactic to good effect. And whilst we're banging the drum for illustration, there's another advantage over photography. The Robinsons campaign and the fish4 ads both have distinctive ideas but they are also executed in distinctive styles. Easier to achieve with illustration and vitally important if you want your brand to stand out in the media clutter.

Yet another advantage of illustration neatly demonstrated by the Robinsons campaign is the idea in **Orange Boy** that orange segments can be transformed into angel's wings. Or that an apple can be turned into a halo in **Apple Halo**.

Or that drops emerging from a watering can could be huge and multi-coloured in **Raise Them on Robinsons**. This wouldn't work nearly as well if attempted photographically. In addition, this illustration style works perfectly when animated so the ads can also live on television, the internet and the increasing numbers of digital posters. A lovely campaign and a great use of illustration.

But back to the Vodafone posters. One of the most visible campaigns of the year, featuring work by Lopetz @Buro Destruct, Mauro Gatti, Andrew Banneker, Nishant Choksi and Adrian Johnson (again). These illustrators have definitely brought a lot to the party, transforming the ads into witty, eyegrabbing and most importantly, memorable pieces of communication. In this case, a consistent but flexible layout ticks the branding box nicely. The different ads sit together well and it's good to see a number of different illustrators' work co-existing within one campaign.

And whilst we're on the highstreet, it would be hard to ignore the impact of grafitti art this year. Well, much of it is illustration. I doubt whether it's practioners are Association of Illustrators members or if they'd consider a commission from a global conglomorate but they now find themselves courted by the fine art world, with crazily escalating prices. So that's also commercial isn't it? And they don't even use a computer.

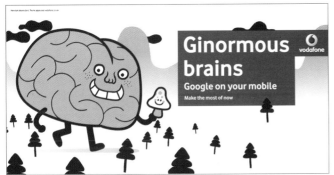

Lopetz @Büro Destruct: Smile

Mauro Gatti: Ginormous

Adrian Johnson: Orange Boy

Andrew Banneker: Lost hour

Nishant Choksi: Wool

Adrian Johnson: Raise Them On Robinsons

Adrian Johnson: Apple Halo

Advertising

Work commissioned for advertising purposes appearing in print and digital media and on posters and television advertising both products and events.

Rosa Apuzzo

Mike Hahn

John McFaul

Philippa Dunning

Sarah Thomson

Judges

Rosa Apuzzo, Senior Art Buyer, Publicis

Rosa Apuzzo graduated from Salisbury Art College, assisted a few photographers for many years, then became a photographers agent representing talent such as Elinor Carucci, Andrew Douglas & Steve Pyke.

She then moved into the world of Art Buying, worked at Saatchi & Saatchi for four years and is now at Publicis for her next challenge. She likes that being an Art Buyer allows her to keep up to date with young up and coming talent.

"The judging was fun and I enjoyed the experience."

Philippa Dunning, Creative Services Director, 23red

Philippa Dunning has been Creative Services Director at 23red for the past 7 years. Before that she ran the creative services department at Tequila for 10 years after originally starting her career as a designer/art director.

Philippa has commissioned illustration across a huge range of brands and medias, picking up a number of illustration awards along the way.

Her team actively encourage the consideration of illustration and ensure the creatives are kept up to speed through arranging trips to illustration galleries and talks.

"I was drawn to those illustrations which expanded on the core idea and drew an emotion which connected with the viewer."

Mike Hahn, Associate Creative Director, Ogilvy NY

Mike Hahn is an Associate Creative Director at Ogilvy New York. Over the last four years he's developed worldwide creative for IBM and Motorola.

Prior to that, he worked at BBH New York and Kirshenbaum Bond and Partners, developing campaigns for clients like Johnny Walker, Target, Axe Body Spray, Men's Journal and Amnesty International. He currently lives in Brooklyn, the finest place on Earth.

"There were so many different styles and techniques among the advertising finalists, but the common thread was clearly a sense of graphic design. The compositions, the palettes, the way each layout invites typography – it's a thin, faint line now separating 'illustrator' and 'designer'. It's what I enjoyed about the work."

John McFaul, Creative Director/The Boss, McFaul Ltd

Instigator of one of the UK's most exciting creative exports, Black Convoy, and now taking the strain as Creative Director of McFaul Ltd, John McFaul and his team have made quite a name for themselves these past few years with a client list including Virgin Atlantic, British Airways, Nike, Adidas and Carhartt.

Their work pushes creative boundaries, and represented in the UK, USA and Dubai, they are gaining an ever increasing global audience.

Comments on winning images:

"Adrian Johnson's Robinsons Ads are quite simply awesome! These Ads are one of the best things I've seen come out of the UK for some time. So charming. Well done to him!"

Sarah Thomson, Art Buyer, DDB London

Sarah is an Art Buyer at DDB London, and prior to this was an Art Buyer at AMV BBDO for five years. After completing a History of Art Degree she worked for a Photographer's Agent, a Photographer and a Gallery before joining AMV.

"I enjoyed judging these awards and the process was made very easy. I thought that some of the work was beautiful and of a very high standard."

Gold

Adrian Johnson

Apple Halo

Medium Mixed media

Brief One of a series of 12 posters and press ads illustrating the strapline 'Raise Them On Robinsons'.

Commissioned by Rosie Arnold

Client BBH

Commissioned for Robinsons

London based illustrator Adrian Johnson draws stuff and sometimes gets paid to do it - a concept he still finds baffling. Amongst his many clients are Paul Smith, Mastercard, Stüssy, Vodafone, The New York Times, 2K, and The Guardian. Described as 'simple, sophisticated, and sometimes plain silly' Johnson's work is 'constantly evolving, juxtaposing satirical wit, [consists of] bold graphic compositions and [has] a unique charm'.

1 Raise
2 Orange boy
3 Sketches
4 Winning illustration

1

2

3

4

Silver

Max Ellis

Tattoo Girl

Medium Digital

Brief Produce a Victorian engraved style image of a London scene for Spanish/US campaign.

Commissioned by Kate Mahon

Client Publicis

Commissioned for Beefeater Gin

Max Ellis left school and trained as an engineer at 17, got bored, got made redundant then took a degree in illustration and photography at Brighton Art College in 1982.

He painted and drew mainly caricatures for ten years for every major publishing house in the UK winning the AOI's 'Best Use of Humour' award in 1992.

In 1997, he lied about having a computer to get a job and switched to digital illustration.

Since then, Max headed ad campaigns for Pro Plus, Halifax bank, O'Neils, Beefeater Gin, Eurostar, Camel fags and Lloyds bank to name but a few.

Currently, he is working on the Bill Bailey tour and website with a tooth abscess....

1 Winning illustration

2 Line drawings

3 Work in context

4 Research

4

Bronze

Chris Haughton

Creating Demand - Not Just Servicing It

Medium Digital

Brief Magazine press advert for a marketing service for MBNA credit card service. 'creating demand, not just servicing it'.

Commissioned by Ken Davies

Client Underdog Creative

Commissioned for MBNA

Chris Haughton is an Irish illustrator living in London. After studying design and illustration in Ireland's National College of Art and Design he settled in Hong Kong for a year and worked freelance doing design and illustration work before moving to London. Chris illustrates for The Guardian, The Independent, The Irish Times and the South China Morning Post.

In 2007, Chris was named in Time magazine's 'Design 100', which listed some of the world's top designers and architects, for the design and illustration work he has been doing for the fair trade company 'People Tree'.

2

1 Winning illustration

2 Rough

3 Rough

3

1

Books

Work commissioned for books, children's books, fiction and non-fiction, book jackets, interior illustrations, graphic novels, natural history and medical etc.

Sara Marafini

Alison Sage

Jonathan Gray

Tamlyn Francis

Eleanor Crow

Judges

Eleanor Crow, Art Director, The Folio Society
Eleanor Crow was a book cover designer at Random House for seven years, before becoming Art Director at the Folio Society in 2007. She has commissioned many illustrators, and has taught on several illustration and graphics courses throughout the UK.

"This winning image was commissioned before I started at Folio; the image was new to me, so I was happy to be able to contribute to the voting."

Tamlyn Francis, Agent, Arena
Tamlyn did a BA in Graphics (illustration) at Norwich graduating in 1992. She felt she wasn't suited to being an illustrator, but loved illustration and found a job in an agency called Sharp Practice in 1993. Two years later she joined Arena and took over at the helm in 2000 and has been running the agency since then. Arena look after over thirty artists and build their careers based around the work that they want to do, from young children's books, to exciting older fiction covers, designs for packaging, advertising work and magazine illustration. It's a varied and challenging role.

"It is very hard to judge interior spreads of a narrative children's book in the same way as a single image for the front cover of a book, so the brief was important to read but I did feel that the children's books illustrators had a harder job to convince the panel that their images were strong enough to deserve a place in our chosen shortlist. We came out with clear winner based on the impact of the piece which I think we all had a strong emotional response to."

Jonathan Gray, Designer/Illustrator/Accountant, gray318
Jonathan Gray designs and illustrates book covers for publishers in the UK, the US and Europe. His illustrations have been published in the Independent, New York Times and New York Magazine.

He currently works in a glorified shed in Hertfordshire.

"Although still very tough to judge, I was surprised at the work that wasn't represented. I guess people are too busy to put their brushes down and bask in their own glory. Or, knowing how tight most illustrators are, they probably couldn't bear to part with the entry fee."

Sara Marafini, Art Director, John Murray Publishers
Sara Marafini studied Graphic Design at Norwich School of Art. She started her career at Penguin Books, and has been Art Director of John Murray for the last 4 years.

"I thought the standard of work this year was very diverse, ranging from the uninspiring to some exceptional pieces featuring strong ideas and interesting compositions. Not all the entries I admired made the shortlist but the judges were unanimous on the winners. Illustrators constantly amaze me with their ability to interpret a brief with originality and innovative thinking."

Alison Sage, Freelance Editor
Alison Sage has spent her working life in children's books. She started in design but became an editor, specialising in picture books and has worked for Harper Collins, Random House and Oxford University Press. As time went on, she tried her hand at writing and also explored different kinds of books, fiction and – most recently – non fiction. She was winner of the children's book of the year for the Hutchinson Treasury of Children's Literature.

"The most difficult thing I found was to decide what criteria to use. Was it what the readers would like – or was it, objectively speaking, the best piece of art on that subject? Was it a good cover, or was it simply a brilliant picture? In the end, I think I compromised a little. The standard of entries was uneven, but what surprised me what how very much in agreement we were about the final line up."

1

Gold

Tom Burns

The New York Trilogy

Medium Mixed media

Brief To Provide 13 full colour illustrations and a binding design for use in a book entitled The New York Trilogy by Paul Auster.

Commissioned by Joe Whitlock-Blundell

Client The Folio Society

Commissioned for The New York Trilogy By Paul Auster

Born in North Yorkshire, England, 1979, Tom Burns moved down to the south west of England to study a degree in Illustration at Exeter College of Art. Since graduating, he spent nearly two years working his way through Europe, South America and Australia. Finally, he ended up back in London to continue his studies at Kingston University and in 2005, graduated with an MA in illustration.

Tom Burns has worked as a freelance illustrator for clients in the UK and US ever since and exhibited photographs, paintings and prints regularly in London. Clients include The Guardian, The Guardian Weekend Magazine, Simplify Design, The Folio Society and John Brown Publishing.

1 Winning illustration

2 Works in progress

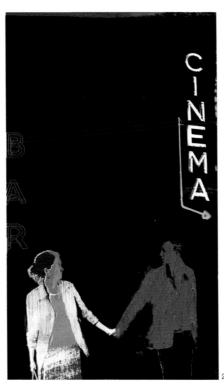

2

1

Portrait by Bish

Silver

Simon Pemberton

Horror Classics - Frankenstein's Monster

Medium Mixed media

Brief Wrap around book cover depicting Frankenstein's Monster through the use of his shadow as a looming presence. Part of 3 book box set.

Commissioned by Conorde Clark

Client Reader's Digest

Commissioned for Reader's Digest Horror Classics

Born near Liverpool Simon moved to London to study BA Hons Design and MA Illustration at Central St Martins College of Art and is now living and working in the East End of London with a studio next to London Fields and an extensive client list across Design, Publishing, Editorial and Newspapers both in the UK and USA.

Clients include Adobe UK, Fuji UK, New York Times, L.A Times, Taylors of Harrogate, Blueprint, Design Week, Guardian, Observer, Independent, Times, Mail on Sunday, Evening Standard, Financial Times, New Scientist, Tatler, VNU Publishing, Future Publishing, Reed Publishing, Penguin Books, Hodder Books, Harper Collins, Random House Publishing, BBC Worldwide...

Simon is the previous winner of an Images Silver award for Editorial work, a Bronze award for Design and New Media and a Bronze for Advertising work.

2

1 Winning illustration

2 Roughs

from **Hereabout Hill**

Giant's Necklace
Ancient Time
Silver Ghost
Muck and Magic

Bronze

Lucy Davey

From Hereabout Hill

Medium Mixed media

Brief To create a cover for the collection of stories by Michael Morpugo, using the poem From Hereabout Hill by Sean Rafferty as inspiration.

Commissioned by Wendy Birch

Client Egmont

Commissioned for Egmont UK

Originally from Exmouth in Devon, Lucy graduated two years ago with a BA in illustration from UWE, Bristol and has now been a fulltime freelance illustrator for just over two years. Lucy was lucky enough to join the Artworks agency after they saw her work at the UWE graduation show in the Coningsby Gallery and since then she has been commissioned in many different areas including editorial, advertising and publishing.

Lucy uses brush and ink, gouache, print and drawing which she then scans separately into Photoshop to create a layered final image – this allows her to move elements of the picture around to find the best composition and change colours easily. Her inspiration comes from many places and she loves the colours of early lithographic prints and railway posters. She also admires the work of artists from the 50's such as Mary Blair and M. Sasek to name a few, as well as contemporary illustration and design.

Lucy has been commissioned for over twenty book covers, many with her own hand lettering, and has worked with several major publishing houses including Wiedenfeld and Nicholson, Transworld, Faber, Quercus and Headline. Other clients include Transport for London, Radio Times, Starbucks, The Guardian and Waitrose Food Illustrated. Lucy still lives and works in Bristol.

1 Winning illustration
2 Sketch

Illustration in the age of Supersized communications
by John O'Reilly

John O'Reilly is a copywriter, editor and writer of visual trend reports for clients including Nike, Virgin Atlantic, Getty Images, the British Council and Playstation. He was a regular contributor on art, music and media for The Guardian and Independent, an editor on Colors Magazine and The Modern Review, and writes for Eye magazine and Varoom. His doctorate in philosophy was on the evolution of the image, and he has taught at Central Saint Martin's, the University of Greenwich and S.U.P.S.I in Switzerland on subjects ranging from psychoanalysis to Ferris Buehler to branding. A book on inspiration and creativity is forthcoming in 2009.

"Drawing is an art of omission". Paul Klee often quoted Max Lieberman's vision of drawing. Great illustration always leaves something out, something unresolved. It's drawing as withdrawing, drawing as holding back, drawing as showing less. It's why in 2008, at a moment dominated by the digital network, in the age of perfect communication, of constant communication, of facebook status updates, illustration's holding back gives it cultural and social charisma.

And perhaps that's the art of great communication, the art of saying less than you need to. In an age of overheated and overcooked communications, of microwave celebrity and instant messaging, illustration can define a space that communicates and blurs at the same time, that gives and takes away.

Like **Lasse Skarbovik**'s poster for the **AOI UP Poster**. Every magazine editor knows to get instant reader connection stick a face on the cover, a pair of staring eyes, and I'm hooked. This poster face is deconstructed into its elements. It's not so much a drawing of a face as the unfolding of one, this person, male or female and both, is growing. It's a fascinating visual metaphor, part human, part plant life, sprouting symbolic gestures and ideas. It's an example of illustration as improvised visual psychology, where a single flourish or a colour or a graphic treatment implies a character trait or entire personality, and this also gives illustration an opening.

Marshall McLuhan argued that the uniformity and repeatability of the printed page and typography gave rise to nationalism. In our current media largely defined by reality tv, social networking and blogs, 'nationalism' is being replaced by 'emotionalism'. We live in an era of 'big emotions' (the 'passion' for football, 'I'm lovin' it' burgers, Big Brother bust-ups) and advertising has been following this trend for big emotions over big ideas, partly because we have somehow managed to confuse big emotions with honesty. What's noticeably compelling about some of the design illustration entries this year is the extent to which their visual power rests on the ability to abstract emotion, to delineate and define, to remove and omit.

Like the curiously spooky romance of the **Twang sleeve**, a bouquet of paranoia, an urban stray, and relationship vertigo. Or the **Truth** image by **Bish** which graphically narrates a story on a torso, with clues scrawled all over the body, but because you don't see the face the clues, don't add up, or at least don't add up to one thing. They are the signs of a random life. It's the awkwardness of the confessional torso that gives this image its ease. The emotional life in these images aren't big as much as they are layered, psychological studies, that don't give everything away.

One of the other trends in the judges choices are visions of nature that are leant a child's perspective, which doesn't mean the adult's view of children – sentimental and sweet. There is the **Meccano Liver Bird** created for the 2008 Liverpool city of culture celebrations. Meccano was originally made in Liverpool and this particular version of the city's symbol is both noble and a little scary. Likewise the **Lemontits** image form the short animation of the same name by **Eleanor Meredith** pictures a slowburning ecological unease, unlike the image for the **Calor Village of the Year 2016** which pictures a soothing candy-coloured toytown, but it's the godlike detail of village life that gives the image such hypnotic charm. And it visualizes an inspiring and childlike dream, that our ecological future lies in community. Just like the **Newington Green** postcard illustration.

Even wine is getting nature's makeover with **Belle Mellor**'s image of people masquerading as the **Ogopogo**, a Canadian mythical beast used on a Wine bottle. This gentle pantomime of nature may suggest a certain mystery behind the wine, a playful wine for easy drinking, but the choice of illustration and execution suggests our current sense of our environment is fluid and ambiguous. **Wendy Plovmand's Wealthywalls** image, illustration as wallpaper nails this in a vertiginous collage of styles, collage itself is a format that signals an inability to visualize a coherent overall picture of how things are.

On the surface of the image itself the exotic animal life sits alongside familiar snatches of wallpaper patterning and disembodied women, while windows and gaps on the surface open out onto another layer of nature. It's a lush psychedelia of blues. It's an unusual piece because wallpaper shouldn't really communicate, it needs to be ambient. You certainly don't want or need your wallpaper to be editorializing your living space, and Plovmand's work sits somewhere between communicating something and communicating nothing.

All these images play to illustration's singular strengths, they cut through the noise of networking and celebrity and relentless communication. And one if illustration captures a trend of where we are in 2008 it is **Tom Gaul**'s illustration of **Basil Fawlty**. It reminded me that Fawlty's popularity wasn't due to the slapstick, or the surreptitious sadistic pleasure in Fawlty's treatment of Manuel, or Fawlty's inept management skills.

The joke relied on Fawlty's character who couldn't communicate, or communicate clearly, and often communicated the exact opposite of what he wanted. Like the image of Fawlty which captures not just the character's unbalanced implosiveness, (for all his famous theatrical rages and explosions, Fawlty was undone from the inside) but the simple lop-sided inability of one half of Fawlty's face to communicate with the other half. Fawlty Towers was a comedy of thwarted communication and Fawlty can't communicate because in Gaul's illustration he sees too much with one eye and not enough with the other, the man is unbalanced.

Fawlty is always unhinged by hiding something, by not communicating and then comically overcompensating by communicating far too much. That's the neck in Gaul's illustration, the point at which Fawlty has overreached. Which is the defining feature of all bad communication – saying too much. (I should probably have taken note of this and stopped after the opening para).

There is a clear cultural and social space for illustration in 2008, a space it is defining and creating for itself. In our supersized communications culture, illustration is an art of omission. And it's the omission that speaks volumes.

Rod Hunt: Calor Village Of The Year 2016

Andy Potts: The Twang – Either Way

Wendy Plovmand: WealthyWalls

Tom Gaul: Basil Fawlty

Belle Mellor: Ogopogos

Bish: Truth

Eleanor Meredith: Lemontits

Chris Vine: Meccano Liver Bird

Jan Bowman: Newington Green

Lasse Skarbovik: Face

Jon Forss

Kjell Ekhorn

Design & New Media

Work commissioned for use in packaging, i.e. record sleeves/ wine labels; calendars; stationery; brochures; catalogues and greeting cards for commercial and private use; merchandising; animation; character development; annual reports; interactive design, i.e. computer games, icons for mobile technology, websites etc.; video, film and television.

Gary Lin

Menno Kluin

Chris Wigan

Ed Webster

Judges

Kjell Ekhorn, Partner, Non-Format (UK)

Kjell Ekhorn was born in Norway, studied graphic design at Central Saint Martins in London where he worked as an independent designer and image-maker before setting up Non-Format with Jon Forss in 2000. They both art direct and design Varoom – the journal of illustration and made images.

"I found judging Images this year rather enjoyable. At the start of the process I questioned myself whether I was getting too exited about a piece of work purely because of personal taste rather than the quality of craftsmanship or the way the brief was answered. However, as the judging went on and I was gaining more of an overview, it became clear that a few pieces really stood out head and shoulders above the rest. I must add that I have seen other great pieces of work produced this year which I would have loved to include but, you can only judge what has been submitted."

Jon Forss, Partner, Non-Format (US)

Jon Forss was raised in rural Gloucestershire, studied Graphic Design at Leicester Polytechnic and eventually moved to London where he hooked up with Kjell Ekhorn to form the creative direction and design team, Non-Format. Together they work on art direction, design and illustration projects for a broad spectrum of clients. In 2007 Forss moved to Minneapolis, USA where he plans to establish a US-based studio for Non-Format. Also in 2007 a hardback monograph entitled Non-Format Love Song was published by Die Gestalten Verlag.

Menno Kluin, Art Director, Saatchi & Saatchi NY

Menno started with Saatchi & Saatchi NY a couple of years ago and was the "most awarded art director worldwide" in 2007 according to Creativity magazine.

He has worked for all the major Saatchi & Saatchi clients including JCPenney, Tide, General Mills, Olay, and Folgers. He has a degree in graphic design from the Graphic Institute in Rotterdam, a bachelor's degree in marketing and communication from InHolland University, and he recently graduated from Miami Ad School Europe with a degree in copywriting and art direction.

Born in Bodegraven, the Netherlands, he currently lives in Brooklyn, New York.

"The winners are fun, storytelling images that are crafted as they should be."

Gary Lin, Head of Design, Still Waters Run Deep

Gary is the head of design at "still waters run deep" an award winning independent branding, design and communications agency with a prestigious client list that includes Sony Ericsson, NetJets, Pret a Manger, PureCircle, British Airways, BBC, and many more both in the UK and globally. He helped to develop a humanist ethos for the "still waters run deep" brand, and is currently working on projects that range from corporate identity to rebranding strategies, and from annual reports to website design. Combining a solid design background in lifestyle, fashion and luxury sectors with experience in running his own fashion business, Gary is passionate about both business and design, especially how companies can be themselves in a beautiful way rather than imposing a visual language for the sake of looking good.

Ed Webster, 4 Creative

Ed started his career at GGT Advertising at the age of 16, where he collected the post and dry cleaning of some of the best art directors in the business. After learning the ropes at various ad agencies, design and production companies, he has been at 4 Creative since 2003.

He commissions art directors, writers, photographers and illustrators and produces off air projects across channel 4's portfolio of channels.

"Judging this year's entries based on my initial feeling of each illustration, compared to taking into account the design brief, I came up with two completely seperate short lists. In consolodating the two, some of my favourite images didn't make the final cut."

Chris Wigan, Head of Creative, Dave

Chris is Head of Creative at the creative business consultancy Dave. Working across a variety of media, and having worked within a range of disciplines, he has found ways to get illustration into most types of project.

He designed and co-created the books 'Change the world for a fiver' and 'Change the world 9-5'. Both of which extolled the virtues of many types of illustration, and went on to nestle in the best sellers lists for a number of weeks.

"There was an impressive diversity amongst all the entries to the awards this year. The winning illustrations reflect this well. All the winners answered the brief with alarming accuracy, and didn't compromise in any way. There was a really welcome freshness and innovation to entries in general. A bumper year."

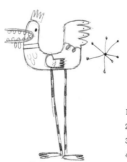

Gold

Steve Simpson

Pure Pie

Medium Digital

Brief To introduce some surrealness into the proceedings, a pie-infused utopia where fascinating creatures live happy lives. To create a range of illustrations that could be used across a range of materials.

Commissioned by Tim Burley

Client Red Rocket

Commissioned for Pure Pie

Steve Simpson grew up in a small town in the heart of Cheshire, England. His keen interest in art was encouraged from an early age and at the age of 15 he landed an exciting opportunity to spend his school holidays working alongside John K Geering, one of the most prolific children's cartoonists in the UK at that time.

Steve then began a more industrial application of his talent when he travelled south to Portsmouth to study Technical Illustration. However, the world of perspective grids and isometric engine cutaways had to survive without Steve's particular talents as he happily threw his pristine rulers and technical pens into the nearby Solent River!

Pencil in hand, he chose instead to embark on a career at a leading Manchester based animation company (where isometric cutaways were rarely required!). Over the next six years at Cosgrove Hall Productions he worked on a wide range of animated classics including Danger Mouse, Count Duckula and Wind in the Willows, as well as the feature film of Roald Dahl's BFG.

In the late 1980s, a rapidly developing Irish animation industry called for Steve's well-honed skills and he moved to work in Ireland as an animator of several TV series including Teenage Mutant Hero Turtles and Budgie the Little Helicopter. His flexibility in technique and ability to work across a range of styles soon saw demand grow for Steve's unique imagery beyond the scope of the animation industry.

Steve now works exclusively as an illustrator. In this field, he can combine his technical training and cartoon background to illustrate for a wide range of creative projects, across the full range of modern media.

1 Winning illustration

2 Print visuals

3 Photos in situ

4 Roughs

1

Silver

Eleanor Meredith

Lemontits

Medium Digital - Flash

Brief A still taken from 'Lemontits' animation.

Commissioned by Aldeburgh Music

Client Aldeburgh Music

Commissioned for Faster than Sound Festival

Eleanor graduated from Duncan of Jordanstone College of Art in 2006 with a BA in illustration and has subsequently been working as a freelance illustrator and animator. Her work has been shown at the Dundee Contemporary Arts Centre, the Baltic, National Media Museum and KOKO amongst others.

Eleanor has recently published a range of her own books and also dabbles in printmaking, live-drawing at concerts and running creative workshops with young people. Recent commissions include the Scottish Executive, Transparent Sound, Camberwell Composers Collective and a mural for a room in the Hotel Bloom in Brussels.

1 Winning illustration

2 Work in context

Bronze

Tom Gaul

Basil Fawlty

Medium Mixed media

Brief To produce a series of illustrations based on classic BBC comedy characters including Basil Fawlty.

Commissioned by Marcus Freeman

Client Marcus Freeman Design

Commissioned for BBC Worldwide

Raised in East London Tom attended the University of the West of England picking up a BA Hons in Illustration along the way, since then he has gradually established a broad client list including BBC Worldwide, Radio Times and The Guardian.

Tom's work is firmly grounded in life drawing, striving to capture likenesses through a range of techniques including constructing computer manipulated collages for reference purposes, and experimenting with various ways of expressive mark making.

Aside from his commercial work, Tom enjoys constantly filling sketchbooks with a variety of found objects, random thoughts and doodles, often using these books to inspire and develop his illustration further. He works and lives in East London.

1 Winning illustration

2 Roughs

1

2

Editorial

Work commissioned for editorial purposes in newspapers, magazines, etc.

Matthew Cook   Daniel Knight

Stefan Ostermeier

Ivan Cottrell

Adrian Shaughnessy

Judges

Matthew Cook, Illustrator, UK
Matthew Cook has worked for nearly 20 years, illustrating for many clients and mostly drawing on location. Recent jobs have taken him to Iraq as The Times War Artist, Afghanistan, N Korea for Conde Nast, Wimbledon as the first Championship artist and on location for Universal Pictures' film of Atonement.

"For the winning image, I instinctively looked for a strong sense of design and use of space, as-well as a clever response to the brief"

Ivan Cottrell, Art Director, Design Week
Ivan is the art director at Design Week magazine and has been for more years than he cares to mention! Even though the magazine largely represents design work there is still a substantial amount of illustration being commissioned both for the main issue and the supplements. Not everything works for Design Week but Ivan does try to give post graduates a chance to be published.

"As well as appreciating style and technique I was also looking for clarity of the idea. Even the simplest of styles can have a stunning effect with a strong well represented idea."

Daniel Knight, Art Director, Bauer: ZOO Magazine
Since starting in editorial design, Daniel has worked on a wide variety of publications and magazine genres: Newspaper supplements, Teen, Women's glossies, and most recently Men's titles (Art directing FHM, FHM Collections and currently ZOO). Through working across such a broad spectrum of magazines, he has enjoyed commissioning a wide variety of illustrations styles – everything from conceptual fashion artwork to informative line-art illustrations.

"Although generally excellent, there was a world of difference between those entrants who 'simply' met their brief (however attractively), and those who took it on to an unexpected level – creating arresting and original images in the process."

Comments on winning images:
Gold: Immediately eye-catching, this truly original graphic image, not only demands the viewers attention, but once gained, invites to re-examine the art-work again and again.
Silver: Although a familiar image, the illustrator brilliantly uses a few 'simple' strokes to completely change the subjects personality – while creating an original image and excellently meeting their brief.

Stefan Ostermeier, Designer and Art Buyer, brand eins, Germany
Stefan Ostermeier studied Graphic Design in Aachen/Germany from 1992 to 1997, then worked on the design of the newly founded magazine ECONY. Since 1999 he has been Designer and since 2002 also Art Buyer for the award winning German magazine brand eins (www.brandeins.de).

"I searched for images I would also like to have in our magazine, which look modern, original and new. Unfortunately there weren't many submissions up to that mark, only few were outstanding.
The winning image (bodyparts) looks modern, and even if the idea is not new, it's graphical transformation is good, funny and self-explanatory."

Adrian Shaughnessy, Freelance Art Director, Designer and Writer
Adrian Shaughnessy is a freelance art director and writer. He is co-founder of design group Intro, and its creative director from 1988-2004. He has written and edited numerous books on visual culture. His most recent work is *How to be a graphic designer without losing your soul*. He is editor of Varoom magazine, writes for all the principal UK design magazines and has a monthly column in Design Week. He is a guest contributor to the blog Design Observer, and hosts a weekly radio show on Resonance FM called *Graphic Design on the Radio*.

"Overall standard was consistently high. No 'bad' work. But, I longed for a bit of rebellion. Some dangerous work!"

Pair of eyes

£ 954

Scalp

£ 380

Face nerve

£ 954

£ 318

Oesophagus

Trachea

£ 318

£ 1,717

Thyroid & Parathyroid

Brain

£	
Amygdala	**£954**
Cerebellum	**£318**
Habenula	**£1,131**
Hippocampus	**£1,131**
Hypothalamus and Pituitary gland	**£2085**
Substantia Nigra	**£954**
Prefrontal Cortex	**£954**
Frontal Cortex	**£318**
Pineal gland	**£954**
Globus Pallidus	**£954**
Thalamus	**£954**
Total	**£10,707**

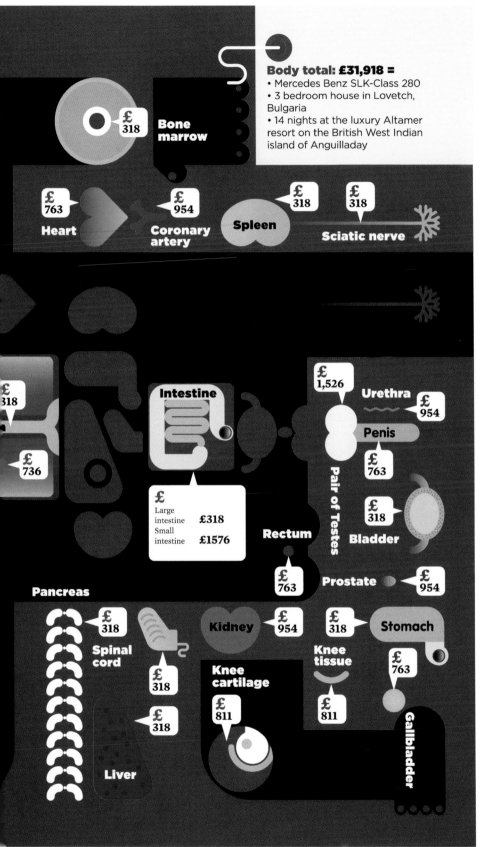

Body total: **£31,918** =
• Mercedes Benz SLK-Class 280
• 3 bedroom house in Lovetch, Bulgaria
• 14 nights at the luxury Altamer resort on the British West Indian island of Anguilladay

£ 318 **Bone marrow**

£ 763 **Heart**

£ 954 **Coronary artery**

Spleen £ 318

£ 318 **Sciatic nerve**

£ 318

£ 736

Intestine

£
Large intestine £318
Small intestine £1576

£ 1,526

Urethra £ 954

Penis

£ 763

£ 318

Bladder

Pair of Testes

Rectum

£ 763

Prostate £ 954

Pancreas

£ 318

Spinal cord

£ 318

£ 318

Liver

Kidney £ 954

£ 318 **Stomach**

Knee tissue

Knee cartilage

£ 811

£ 811

£ 763

Gallbladder

Gold

Peter Grundy

Bodyparts

Medium Digital
Brief Diagram to explain the cost of your body parts.
Commissioned by Alex Breuer
Client Esquire Magazine

In 1975, while a student at the then 'Bath Academy of Art' Peter's drawing tutor sauntered up to him in a life drawing class, looked at what he was doing and said, 'It takes 30 years to create a style'.

Well, over the last three decades Peter has indeed created a distinctive style.

He attended the school of Graphic Design at the RCA in the late 70s, then formed one half of the information design team, Grundy & Northedge, which lasted for 26 years and most recently, he has incarnated himself as Grundini.

His work is about explaining things, sometimes complex, sometimes not, mostly for clients, sometimes for customers, always for himself.

Peter simplifies what he thinks and sees by using icons, symbols and pictograms as vehicles to carry ideas that form visual messages.

Information design and illustration do not have to be boring.

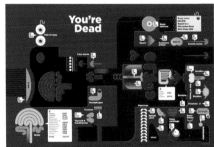

1

2

1 Winning illustration

2 Visual

Silver

Phil Disley

Mad Churchill

Medium Pen & ink, pastels and Photoshop

Brief To illustrate a piece about mental illness and how it can effect the great and good.

Commissioned by Andrew Spocks

Client The Guardian

It all started for Phil when he was about five. One of his earliest and most embarrassing memories is that of hawking around a plastercine Lone Ranger and Silver to the Headmaster and numerous classes in his infant school.

In a bizarre way he must have enjoyed that cringed feeling and still does to this day when people recognise and comment on his drawings.

Phil meandered through Secondary School and a Diploma from Liverpool's Foundation of Art followed. He went on to obtain a place at Newcastle studying Graphics.

He knew early on he wanted to pursue illustration and was fortunate to have Terry Dowling as the course leader. Newcastle was great and the course had some fantastic guest lecturers including Steven Appleby, Bush Hollyhead and George Hardie who really opened his eyes.

Phil completed the course with the obligatory Desmond 2:2, which he believes, means he had enjoyed himself. He left with a mish-mash of a folio, which contained, quote "some interesting stuff"!

His first commission was for 'The Big Issue' in 1993. The illustration was noticed by the Creative Director of the 'Evening Standard' and his career began. For the next three years Phil was a regular contributor to the 'Standard' and since then he has been fortunate enough to work for some of the most prestigious titles both here and in America.

Phil's work can be seen in 'The Times', 'The Guardian', 'Financial Times', 'GQ', 'Classic FM', 'Decanter' and 'The Tablet'.

1 Winning illustration

2 Rough

1

2

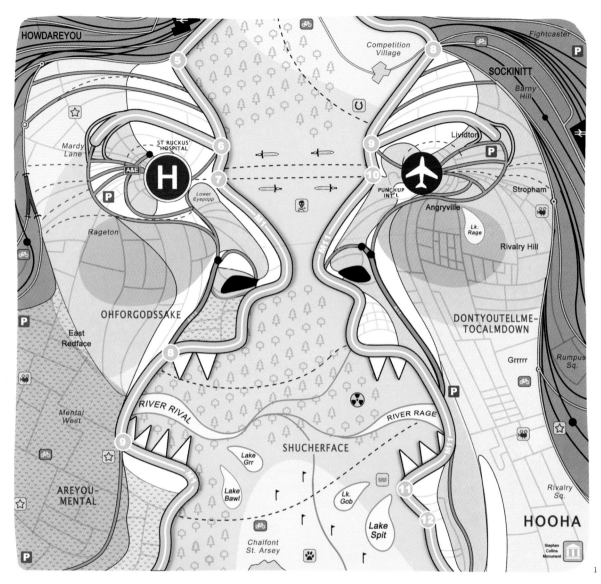

1

Bronze

Stephen Collins

Competition Between Cities

Medium Digital

Brief Cities compete for funding and raised profiles.

Commissioned by Jeremy Vine

Client The Times

Commissioned for The Times

Stephen Collins was born in East Dulwich, South London in 1980. His first drawing was of a chocolate biscuit. At school he developed a love of caricature and cartoons but despite childhood ambitions to become a cartoonist he opted to study literature and philosophy at University. It wasn't until he started contributing cartoons to his student newspaper at the University of East Anglia that he considered illustration as a viable career. After winning a student journalism award and working as a features researcher for The Times, a few very brave editors agreed to let him provide illustrations alongside his written work. He spent the next year working days as a researcher and nights drawing cartoons, before deciding in 2003 to follow what he loved and become a freelance illustrator.

Since then his client base has included most major British broadsheets, and many magazines including GQ, NME, Gay Times, Word, The Big Issue, FHM and Q. His weekly comic strip 'The Day Job', appears in The Times Career section every Thursday.

His work broadly divides between cartoons, caricature and general editorial commissions. He works up pencil roughs digitally, mostly using Photoshop. In all his work he is constantly racking his brains for new and inventive ways of presenting information, whether that is a joke, a topical issue, or a subject's personality. His caricature seeks to maintain a dimension of depth and portraiture, whilst his comic strips display a wordy, surreal humour more commonly associated with comedy.

He thinks that Gary Larson, Ralph Steadman, Peter Cook, a bit of Chris Ware and lots of Radio 4 have something to do with the current state of his life.

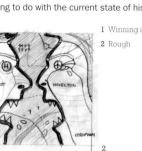

1 Winning illustration

2 Rough

2

Self Promotion

Unpublished experimental work and personal promotional work, including speculative
publishing projects and work rejected or not used by a client.

Raquel Leis Allion

Laura Carlin

Marie O'Connor

Gina Cross

Dirk Rehm

Judges

Laura Carlin, Illustrator, UK
Laura Carlin is both a freelance illustrator and part time lecturer. She is involved with the planning of the Museum of Illustration – the world's first – to be housed in London.

She thinks that while illustration is becoming more and more popular and has the possibility of becoming increasingly exciting and challenging, it's also in danger of becoming more and more diluted. For the winners she was looking for personality and enthusiasm in a successful image.

"I enjoyed marking the competition and, as ever, the competition attracted accomplished and strong artists. I was however quite surprised by the lack of personality in a lot of the images. While illustration should communicate, I think we should do everything we can to not merge our visuals into one style and forget to enlighten or intrigue people. Nor should we patronise the audience with carefully spelt out scenarios. It made the choice of winners a fairly easy task since they were the ones where the artists looked as though they were enjoying the process of image making."

Gina Cross, Art and Design Manager, The Guardian Newspaper
Gina originally studied Printed Textiles at Middlesex University and has previously worked in fashion and interior decoration. As the Guardian's Art and Design manager, she is the main point of contact for illustrators on the paper and commissions regularly. Over the past few years she has built up very good relationships with regular contributors and is responsible for introducing new illustration work to designers and art directors at the Guardian. She regularly visits colleges to talk about editorial illustration and self-promotion with students. Gina also works freelance as an agent and curator.

"Self-promotion is crucial to any illustrator's success. There was a very mixed bag of styles and expertise in the competition, some of it quite amateur and others that were highly professional which made judging quite hard. I therefore set myself a criteria to ask myself when judging the entries whether the illustrator was communicating their style effectively and in a relevant way. I found this useful as a tool to judge work fairly, rather than being based on whether I found it visually pleasing or not."

Comments on winning images:
This year's winners in the Self-Promotion category stood out purely on the quality of the work, with strong evidence of the illustrators having good concepts and being able to execute them to a very high standard.

Raquel Leis Allion, Designer, Little, Brown Book Group
Raquel has worked in publishing for the past 10 years both in-house and freelance. Currently working for Little, Brown Books UK she works on a varied list from literary & popular fiction, biographies, non fiction right through to some sci-fi and teenage fiction. Most covers require illustration and she has lots of experience commissioning, which is part of what she loves about her job.

"The way I judged the top ten was to mark my favourite as the most original one. Working in publishing I get to see a lot of illustrators. Some of the work in the top selection I had already seen before. For the self-promotion piece you really have to stand out amongst the rest & there is definitley one there. Saying that, all of the selected ten were of a real high standard."

Marie O'Connor, Illustrator, Peepshow Collective
Designer, illustrator and fashion consultant Marie O'Connor works on collaborative and independent projects, building a diverse folio of work across a range of disciplines. She continues to receive illustration commissions for many magazines and advertising campaigns internationally and she has exhibited in London, Hamburg and New York.

Also, as a member of London collective "Peepshow" she works on illustration and animation projects, site-specific customisation of spaces and group shows.

Marie is a visiting tutor for many institutions nationwide, including Camberwell College of Arts & Crafts in London and Glasgow School of Art.

"It was a huge privilege to judge the AOI's self-promotion award. I found it quite a difficult task as there were many interesting takes on wide-ranging subject matter and the sensibilities of each varied greatly! I felt the best submissions were playful in their image-making, and hope a more experimental approach can continue in the work of all those who entered."

Dirk Rehm, Publisher, Reprodukt, Germany
Since the early Nineties Dirk Rehm has been publishing comic books from around the world at Reprodukt. At his own publishing company he produces German tranlsations of illustrious artists as Charles Bruns, Daniel Clowes, Julie Doucet, Los Bros Hernandez or David Mazzucchelli to name just a few. Besides publishing he keeps working as a hand letterer, a profession dying out since digitalization took over (still the best publishing houses in comics like Drawn and Quarterly, Montreal or L´Association, Paris are trying hard to maintain a special quality to their books and he's got a lot of jobs coming in.)

"Illustrators are back on top with skillful techniques and intelligent ideas."

Gold

A. Richard Allen

Tick Tock

Medium Pencil, acrylic and digital

Brief Self-promotional piece to combine serene graphic elements with an implied narrative and a hint of menace.

A. Richard Allen studied Fine Art as an undergraduate at Central Saint Martins College in London. After some dawdling and a stint as an administrator he went on to gain a Masters degree in illustration from the same college.

Since turning freelance in 2001, Richard has been commissioned by a wide range of clients in the US and Europe including The NY Times, The Wall St Journal, The New Yorker, Plansponsor, The New Statesman, The Independent, The Guardian, The Times, Reader's Digest and The FT. Richard has also worked with numerous advertising and design clients.

Richard won the Gold Award for Editorial in Images 31, a Gold Medal from the Society of Illustrators (LA) and a Silver from the Society of Illustrators (NY).

Richard lives in Bournemouth with his wife and children.

1 Sketch

2 Winning illustration

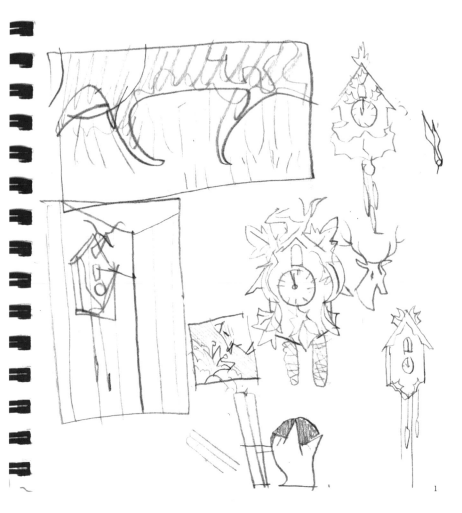

1

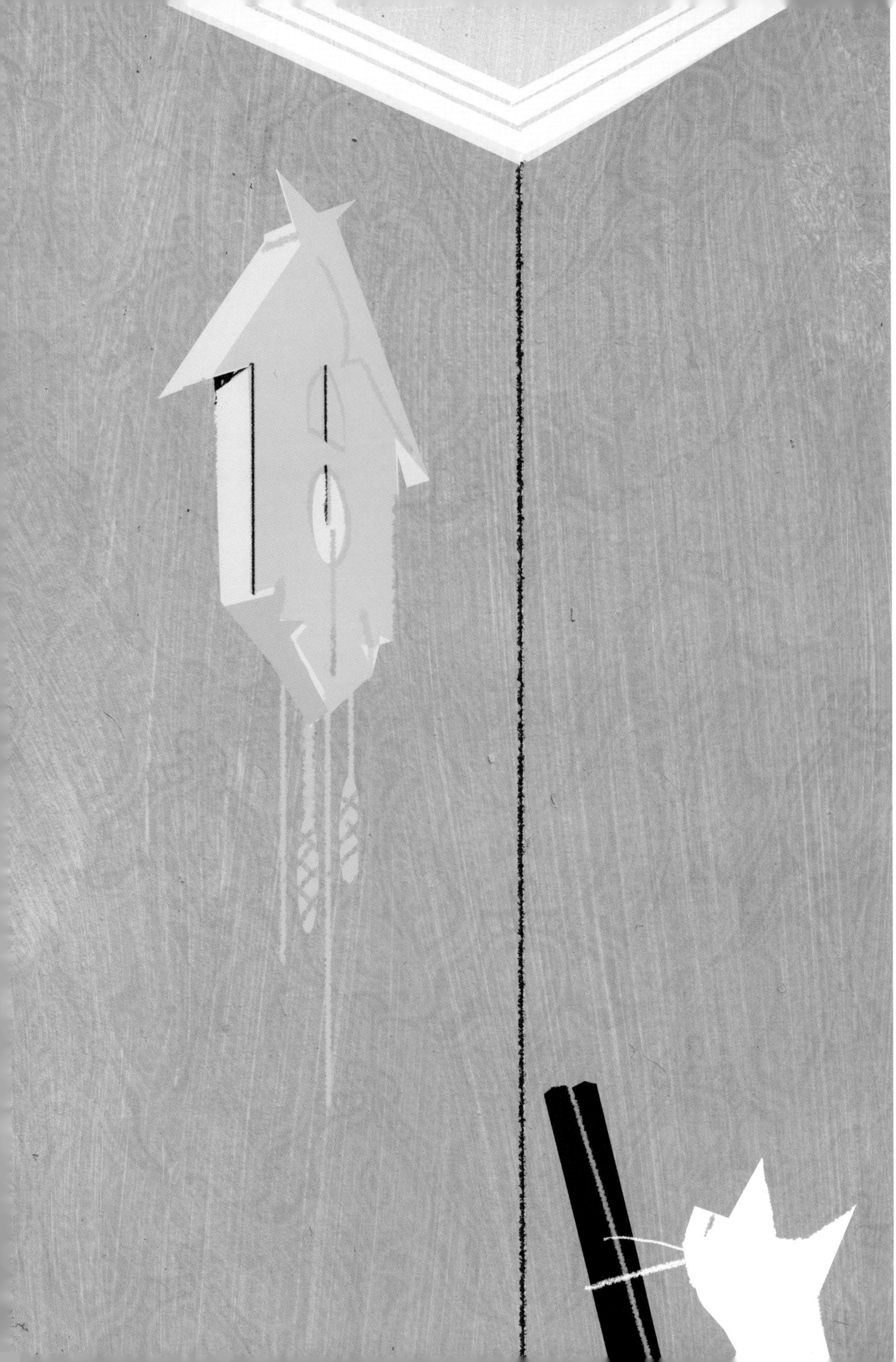

2

Silver

Caroline Tomlinson

Happy 1st Birthday Jelly

Medium Collage

Brief Create an image to celebrate illustration agent Jelly's first birthday.

Commissioned by Charlie Sells

Client Jelly

Caroline Tomlinson graduated from Norwich School of Art and Design in 2000 and then went on to complete her MA at Central Saint Martins. Since graduating she has worked both full time and freelance as an illustrator and designer.

Her work consists of collage, which is made from found papers, old photographs and both hand drawn and painted elements. This is in an effort to prevent the work looking too much like a 'computerised creation' whilst finding beauty in the imperfections of the materials she works with. During her time as a designer Caroline was inspired by typography, an influence, which is apparent throughout her illustrations.

Caroline's images have featured predominantly within editorial publication. She has also produced pieces for publishing, design and advertising. Caroline has worked with numerous clients both in the US and the UK including The Guardian, Royal Mail, Wieden and Kennedy, Meredith Publishing and The Home Office.

In 2006, she was short-listed for "New Arrivals. New Voices in Illustration", an exhibition of illustrators brought together by the Coningsby Gallery. Judges considered her work to have a fresh style and approach that would make a significant contribution to illustration over the coming years.

In early 2008, Caroline's work travelled across the pond to appear in an exhibition in New York City held by '3x3 Magazine - Contemporary Illustration Show'. This annual exhibition showcases carefully chosen work, which is considered to push the boundaries of contemporary illustration.

Caroline lives and works in London keeping her eyes peeled for any old photographs that might come her way.

Bronze

Chris Vine

Manhattan Landscape

Medium Acrylic

Brief An image describing how Manhattan Island might have looked - but for the Pilgrim Fathers.

After lecturing full-time in art at Cumbria College of Art and the Cockpit Theatre, London, Chris Vine became a freelance artist/illustrator from 1983 onwards.

Much of his work revolves around visual language. He uses visual figures-of-speech; mixed metaphors, contradictions, palindromes, paradoxes and clashing clichés, to humourously describe both the real and the imagined.

Chris has exhibited his work widely, amongst others at the 'Drawn to Humour' show at Cleveland Art Gallery, at the Museum of Humour and Satire, Gabrovo, Bulgaria, at the Hourglass Gallery, Paris, the Slaughterhouse Gallery, Liverpool, and at the Chelsea Arts Club in London.

Clients include Cook School, Radio Times, Sunday Times, Sunday Telegraph, Guardian, Wire, Saturday Night (Toronto), Illustrated London News, BT, Yamaha, JWT, Y&R, Collins, Cassells, Larousse, Octopus, Arrow, Northern Broadsides Theatre, HBOS.

Currently, Chris is undertaking a major painting commission for Liverpool 2008, European Capital of Culture.

1 Winning illustration
2 Sketches
3 Colour study

Critic's Award by Alice Rawsthorn

Alice Rawsthorn is the design critic of the International Herald Tribune, writing a weekly column on innovations in design and its impact on our lives. She also writes the Object Lesson column for the New York Times Magazine. Alice sits on the board of Arts Council England, and is a trustee of the Whitechapel Gallery in London. From 2001 to 2006, she was director of the Design Museum and, before then, an award-winning journalist with the Financial Times. Her books include an acclaimed biography of the fashion designer Yves Saint Laurent, and a monograph on the designer Marc Newson.

Rosemary Squire
Gordon Brown's Record As Chancellor

If you look up the word "illustration" in the OED, the first definition you'll find is "illumination (spiritual, intellectual, or physical), the second "the action of making or fact of being made illustrious", and the third "the action or fact or making clear or evident". It's not until you come to the fourth and final one that you'll hit upon the subject matter of this book: "the pictorial elucidation of any subject".

It all sounds rather grand, and surprisingly reverential given that the history of British illustration is drenched in satire: sometimes bawdy, sometimes political, but unfailingly irreverent. And my chosen illustration for the Critic's Award is an intriguing addition to that tradition – Rosemary Squire's depiction of Gordon Brown's Record As Chancellor.

Being asked to give a prize to something just because you like it – rather than because it conforms to a specific set of criteria – is both enticing, and mildly terrifying. I went about it in the hopefully fair, but unscientific manner of picking the illustrations I liked best (no easy task given that there were so many great contenders), and choosing the one I'd be least likely to forget.

That turned out to be Rosemary Squire's vision of Gordon Brown clambering up a tree clad in a plush velvet suit, one hand clutching a ministerial red box stuffed with crumpled twenties, his teeth grimacing into the eerie smile he sports to avoid being papped when looking less than blithely optimistic. Shouting to him for help beneath the tree are the peasants he is abandoning to fend for themselves in the economic debris of his reign as Chancellor.

Rosemary Squire graduated from Loughborough University in 2007 with a BA Honours degree in Illustration. Since then she has spent time working in the puppet department of the West End production of the Lion King. Recent work has won critical acclaim and a place in the 2007 REFRESH! exhibition.

Rosemary's broad spectrum of talents includes the use of digital media, image manipulation, collage and 3D modelling to produce her illustrations, and her passion for observing people is reflected in her models. Her aim is to engage people's interest in her work through the use of satire and humour. She develops her characters' personalities through the careful selection and use of a wide range of media.

Further examples of Rosemary's work can be viewed at www.rosemary-squire.co.uk.

1

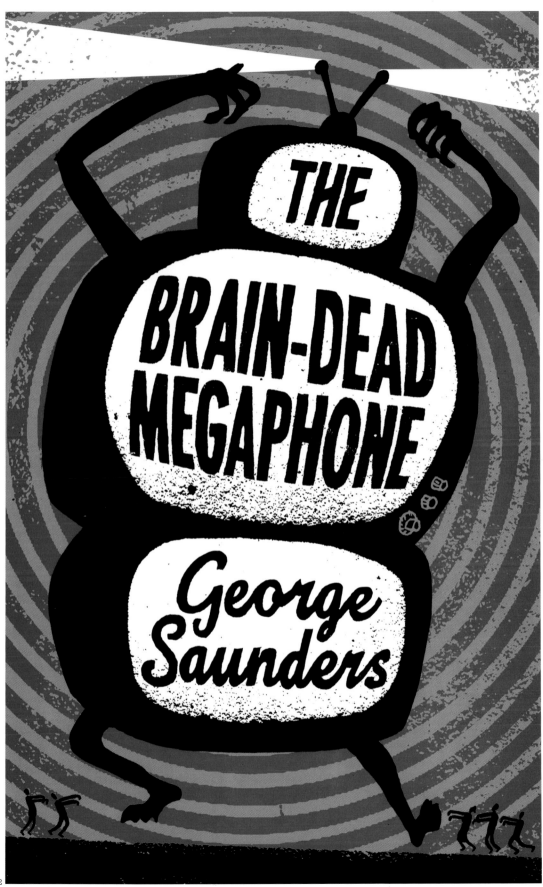

Andy Smith

1. Reverend Guppy

Section Books

Medium Digital

Brief Illustrate the book jacket
using 'fishing' scenes.

Commissioned by Juliet Rowley

Client Random House

Commissioned for
Random House

2. The Brain-Dead
Megaphone

Section Books

Medium Digital

Brief Create a cover illustration
featuring a 'TV Monster'
controlling the viewers, as
refered to in the title of the book.

Commissioned by Sarah Morris

Client Bloomsbury

Commissioned for Bloomsbury

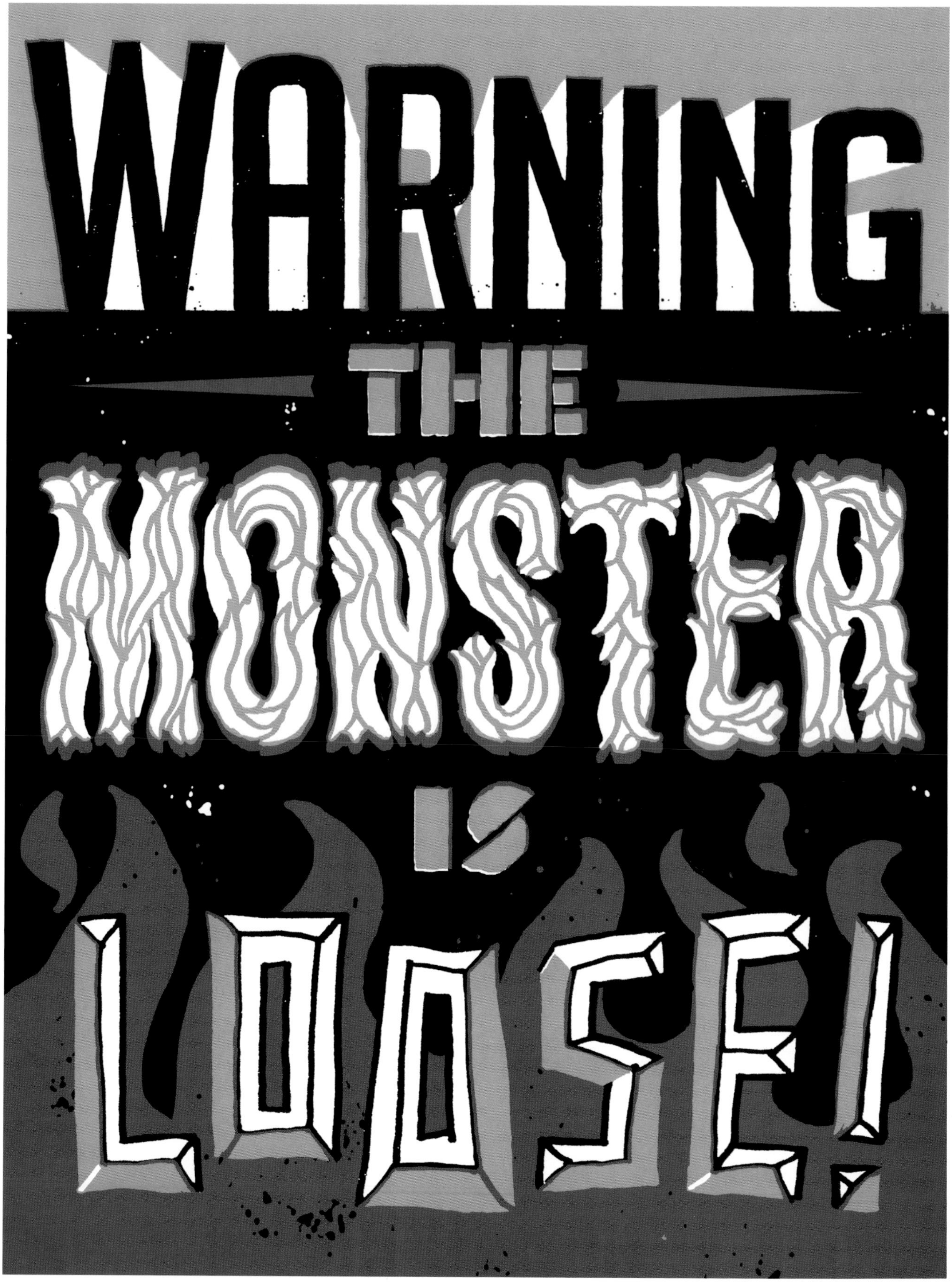

1

Andy Smith

1. Warning - The Monster Is
   Loose

Section Self-promotion

Medium Silkscreen

Brief Create a promotional poster to mail out
to clients at Halloween.

Adrian Valencia

2. Women & Dogs

Section Self-promotion

Medium Pen and digital

Brief One in a series of greetings cards.
Women and dogs. Stylish and humorous
piece. The women have to have similarities
with their dogs preferably: Great Dane, fox
terrier, Doberman, Chihuahua, gundog and
point dog.

1

2

Paul Blow

1. Broken English

Section Editorial

Medium Digital

Brief A distraught 13-year-old Kurdish refugee in Britain is removed from her home in Kent and incaracerated in a detention centre. Her only company is a butterfly as she lives in conditions that shame our nation.

Commissioned by Ped Millichamp

Client Radio Times

Commissioned for Radio Times

2. The School Holidays

Section Editorial

Medium Digital

Brief To Illustrate an article about the problems faced by parents once the schools break up for the holiday's.

Commissioned by Stephen Petch

Client Indpendent

Commissioned for The Independent Magazine

Tim Bradford

3. The Event Poster

Section Advertising

Medium Digital

Brief To create a poster for "The Event" a micro festival targeted at young people.

Commissioned by Sarah Sharpe

Client St. Lukes Church

Music from **electralyte**

Speaking from **ANDREW CROFT**

the EVENT

2 Till 9 PM

SAT 21st APRIL KEYWORTH PLAYING FIELD

Keyworth Churches in partnership with St. Lukes Church West Bridgford

Artwork: timbrad.co.uk

Nishant Choksi

1. Würstchen

Section Self-promotion

Medium Digital

Brief Part of an alphabet series using food as the theme.

2. Perking Up A Workforce

Section Editorial

Medium Digital

Brief Employers are finding that holiday entitlements, pensions and even a share of the profits are key to attracting and retaining staff.

Commissioned by Simon Eastwood

Client Printweek

Valérie Pézeron, aka Valoche

Heroes

Section Editorial

Medium Mixed media

Brief To illustrate an article about French anti-globalisation activist José Bové and his fight against Mc Donald's and the fast food industry.

Commissioned by Michelle

Client Don't Panic Online

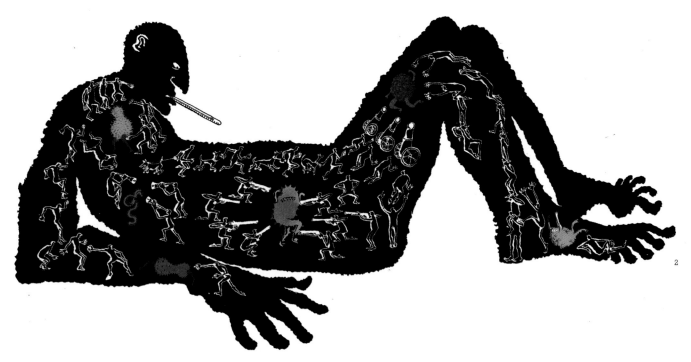

Belle Mellor

1. Ogopogos

Section Design

Medium Pen, ink and digital

Brief Images of people pretending to be The Ogopogo, a Canadian mythical beast, to be printed on a Wine bottle.

Commissioned by Bernie Hadley Beauregard

Client Brandever Strategy Inc

Commissioned for Monster Cellars

2. Immune System

Section Editorial

Medium Pen, ink and digital

Brief For an article on the functioning of the immune system.

Commissioned by John Edney

Client Canadian Living Magazine

3. Twig Model

Section Editorial

Medium Pen, ink and digital

Brief For an article commenting on twig-like models and the daft creations they wear.

Commissioned by Izabella Bielawska

Client The Guardian

Belle Mellor

1. Festival Of Beards

Section Self-promotion

Medium Pen & ink

Brief One of a series of images on the theme of unusual festivals, for a promotonal book produced my agent, Three in Box.

3

4

Chris Vine

2. Meccano Liver Bird

Section Design

Medium Acrylic

Brief An image to represent an aspect
of Liverpool's history and culture for the
Liverpool 2008 celebrations. Meccano was
originally made in Liverpool.

Commissioned by Alex Corina

Client Artworks Liverpool

Commissioned for Artworks Liverpool

3. Duck Meets The Fox

Section Books

Medium Ink and watercolour

Brief Illustration for 'The girl who swallowed
the wind'. - A duck, a rook and a fox form an
unlikely alliance to find the missing wind.

Commissioned by Barrie Rutter

Client
Northern Broadsides Theatre Company

Commissioned for
Northern Broadsides Publications

4. Malvolio's Folly

Section Design

Medium Ink and watercolour

Brief Malvolio - Shakespeare's 'Twelfth
Night' - falls hopelessly in love and loses all
reason. His heart overrules his head. A visual
metaphor for Malvolio's condition.

Commissioned by Sue Andrews

Client
Northern Broadsides Theatre Company

Commissioned for
Northern Broadsides Publications

1

2

Gail Armstrong

1. Receipt Horse

Section Advertising

Medium Paper sculpture

Brief A strong and powerful work horse made
entirely of till receipts, reflects the speed, strength
and reliability of the TGP till printer advertised.

Commissioned by Jason Smith

Client Erwin-Penland Advertising

Commissioned for TGP

3

4

Philip Wrigglesworth

2. Laughable Loves/ Milan Kundera

Section Self-promotion

Medium Collage

Brief To create a cover for Milan Kundera's book of short stories looking into the concept of love.

3. Behaviour Patterns

Section Self-promotion

Medium Mixed media

Brief A self- initiated study into the behavioural patterns in children and the decisions they make naturally.

4. Panicology

Section Books

Medium Collage

Brief The brief was to illustrate a book called Panicology, which looked into scaremongering stories.

Commissioned by Steve Marking

Client Penguin

Commissioned for Panicology

Russell Cobb

1. Cut Down In
 One's Prime

Section Self-promotion

Medium Mixed media

Brief From a body on
work about emotions
experienced within the
human condition.

2. Positive
 Thinking

Section Self-promotion

Medium Mixed media

Brief From a body on
work about emotions
experienced within the
human condition.

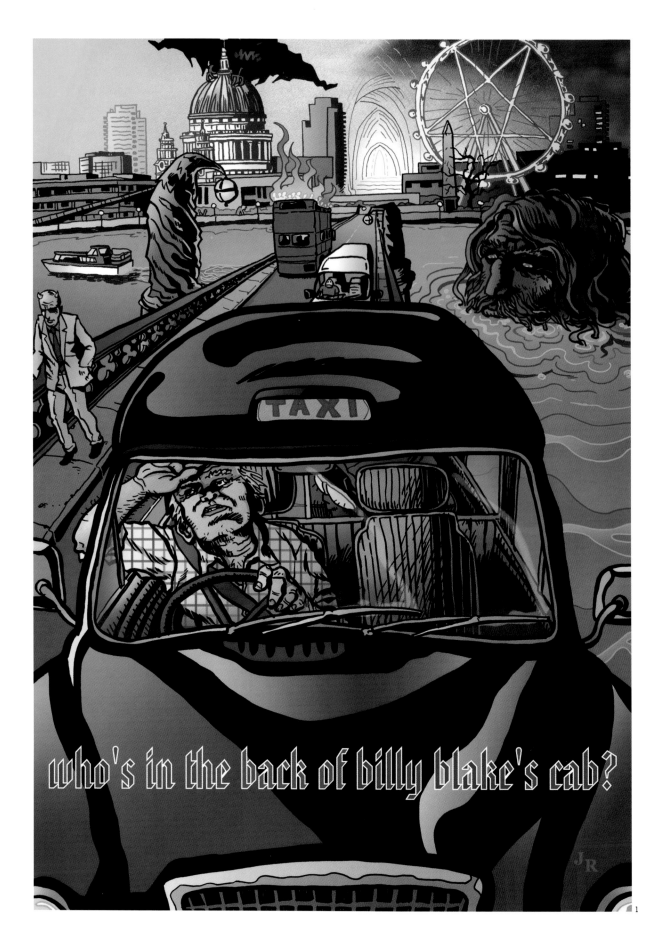

Dominic Harman

2. Northern Lights

Section Books

Medium Digital

Brief Cover for the first book of the trilogy by Philip Pullman

Commissioned by Andrew Biscomb

Client Scholastic Children's Books

3. The Subtle Knife

Section Books

Medium Digital

Brief Cover for the second book of the trilogy by Philip Pullman.

Commissioned by Andrew Biscomb

Client Scholastic Children's Books

4. The Amber Spyglass

Section Books

Medium Digital

Brief Cover for the third book of the trilogy by Philip Pullman.

Commissioned by Andrew Biscomb

Client Scholastic Children's Books

John Riordan

1. William Blake, Taxi Driver

Section Self-promotion

Medium Pen, ink and Photoshop

Brief Promotional image for pitching William Blake, Taxi Driver comic strip to Time Out magazine.

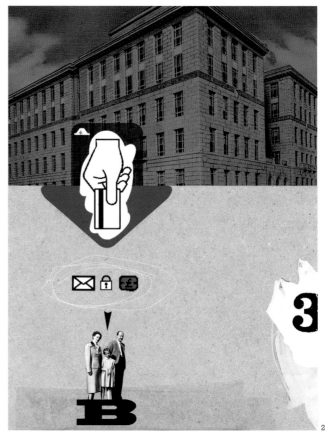

Caroline Tomlinson

1. When She Was Queen

Section Editorial

Medium Collage

Brief Create an illustration to accompany the short story 'When She was Queen'. The text is open to interpretation.

Commissioned by Jo Phillips

Client Transmission Magazine

Commissioned for Transmission Magazine

2. Royal Mail Secure Business Mail

Section Editorial

Medium Collage

Brief Royal Mail has a new service Secure Business Mail. This will protect important packages, such as credit cards and will help prevent fraud.

Commissioned by Richard Murray

Client Redwood Group

Commissioned for Royal Mail Contact magazine

4

5

Caroline Tomlinson

3. Working From Home

Section Editorial

Medium Collage

Brief Illustrate an article which highlights the benefits of the increasing trend of working from home.

Commissioned by Richard Murray

Client Redwood Group

Commissioned for
Royal Mail Contact Magazine

4. Fairtrade?

Section Editorial

Medium Collage

Brief Illustrate feature about Fairtrade. Specifically whether money can be made from it rather than Fairtrade just being altruistic.

Commissioned by Erroll Jones

Client Caspian Publishing Ltd

Commissioned for Real Business Magazine

5. Under Construction

Section Self-promotion

Medium Collage

Brief Create an image that depicts Under Construction for Wieden and Kennedy. To appear as hoarding outside their London studio on Brick Lane during rebuilding work.

Commissioned by Joanna Borton

Client Wieden & Kennedy

Commissioned for
Wieden & Kennedy Hoarding

Ian Whadcock

1. Education Guardian Improbable Research 'Laundry Marks'

Section Editorial

Medium Digital and mixed media

Brief In a laundry - how do people behave. Sociologist camps out in middle class laundry and takes detailed notes. Soapsuds, space and sociability.

Commissioned by John-Henry Barac

Client The Guardian

Commissioned for G2 Education

2. Managing Differences

Section Editorial

Medium Digital and mixed media

Brief Global strategy to manage differences that occur at borders between countries and markets. The world is not flat in terms of economics and it is addressing the borders that create opportunities for profit.

Commissioned by Annette Trivette

Client Harvard Business Review

Commissioned for Harvard Business Review

3. Commercial Property - How To Invest And Beat The Taxman

Section Editorial

Medium Digital and mixed media

Brief Investors Chronicle focus on Real Estate Investment Trusts (REITS) - in a recent deal the taxman has taken a one off 10% charge - which means investors get to share 90% of the profits.

Commissioned by Erica Morgan

Client FT Business

Commissioned for Investors Chronicle

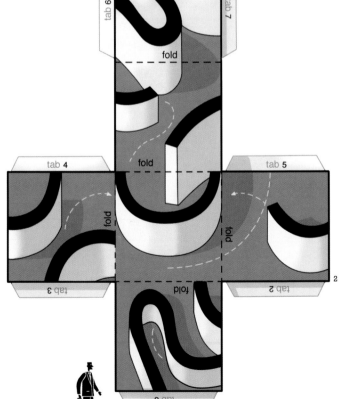

CIA

Alan Aldridge Tom Bagshaw **Andrew Bannecker** Jonas Bergstrand **Bertie Bib** Ian Bilbey **Sir Peter Blake** Bernard Blatch **Stephen Bliss** Louise Brierley **Christopher Brown** Mick Brownfield **Lesley Buckingham** Andrew Bylo **Leonello Calvetti** Stanley Chow **Haydn Cornner** Dust **Tristan Eaton** Max Ellis **Jeff Fisher** Jessie Ford **Andrew Foster** Jonathan Gibbs **Chris Gilvan Cartwright** Brian Grimwood **Lynden Gold** Martin Haake **Olaf Hajek** Tomer Hanuka **Johnny Hardstaff** Sara Hayward **Fine & Dandy** Fiona Hewitt **David Holmes** Peter Horridge **Frazer Hudson** David Hughes **Thorbjorn Ingason** M.H. Jeeves **Adrian Johnson** Kai & Sunny **Chris Kasch** Anja Kroencke **Jacqueline Mair** Jimi Mackay **Tina Mansuwan** Tim Marrs **Mick Marston** Mcfaul **Clare Melinsky** Kate Miller **Mitch** Karen Murray **Dave Needham** Fabian Negrin **Gary Neill** Paul Oakley **Kristian Olson** Nigel Owen **Jackie Parsons** Jitesh Patel **Ulla Puggaard** Maria Raymondsdotter **Harriet Russell** John Royle **Jeremy Sancha** Michael Sheehy **Paul Slater** John Spencer **Simon Spilsbury** Ray Smith **Louisa St. Pierre** Symbolon **Mark Thomas** Benjamin Wachenje **Russell Walker** Fiona White **Mike Wilks**

PAVO REAL
by Patricia Urquiola for Driade

Jonas Bergstrand

1. CIA Boxer

Section Advertising

Medium Mixed media, digital, Illustrator and Photoshop

Brief Image promoting the Central Illustration Agency.

Client Central Illustration Agency

Commissioned for Central Illustration Agency

2. Adieu Magny Cours

Section Editorial

Medium Digital, Illustrator and Photoshop.

Brief Cover image for The Red Bulletin. Magazine devoted to Formula 1 racing. Main story: last race ever on the French track Magny Cours.

Commissioned by Miles English

Client The Red Bulletin

Commissioned for The Red Bulletin

3. Sophia Loren/Pavo Real

Section Self-promotion

Medium Digital, Illustrator and Photoshop.

Brief Image made free of charge, in self interest, for the Italian Design Agency, IDA.

Client IDA, Italian Design Agency

4. Living With Schizophrenia

Section Editorial

Medium Mixed media, digital, Illustrator and Photoshop.

Brief A full page image relating to the difficulties of living with schizophrenia.

Commissioned by Polly Butterfield

Client Saga Magazine

Commissioned for Saga Magazine

Trevor Lake MA

1. The Peppergreen Twins

Section Self-promotion

Medium Illustrator

Brief One in a series of contemporary illustrations, produced for children's story book.

2. A Summer To Remember

Section Self-promotion

Medium Illustrator

Brief One in a series of contemporary illustrations, produced for self promotion.

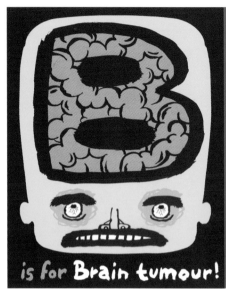  

is for **Brain tumour!**   is for **Asthma!**   is for **Dry Eyes!**

1

wads of fivers wrapped in rubber-bands and **THEN** flung into a

fURnace

2

GRRRRRR!

3

Kenneth Andersson

1. A-Z Hypocondric

Section Editorial

Medium Digital

Brief From a series of illustrations for A-Z Hypocondric article series.

Commissioned by Richard Keenan

Client Time Out Magazine

2. Furnace

Section Editorial

Medium Digital

Brief Illustrating a poem and using the text in the illustration.

Commissioned by Sarah Lomax

Client Dreams that Money Can Buy

3. Big Dog

Section Self-promotion

Medium Digital

Brief For a children's book "ABC och hör" (ABC and listen).

1

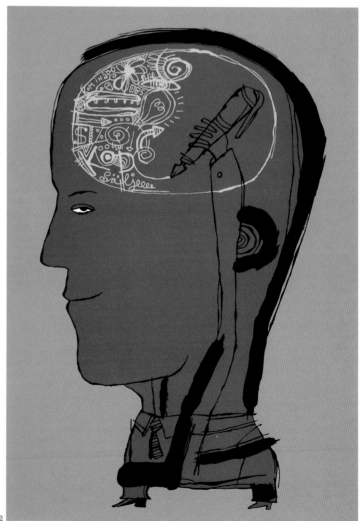

2

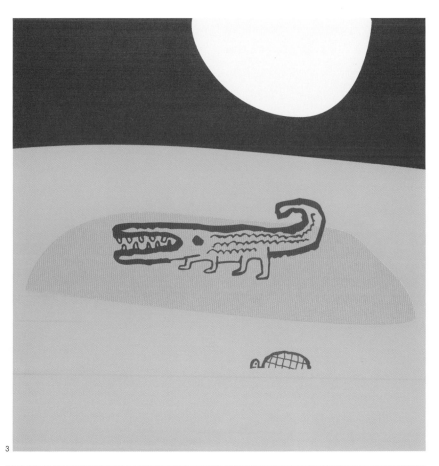

Kenneth Andersson

1. Diego!

Section Self-promotion
Medium Digital
Brief About living as a student.

2. Untitled

Section Self-promotion
Medium Digital
Brief About creativity.

3. Turtle2

Section Self-promotion
Medium Digital
Brief Personal work.

4. Turtle3

Section Self-promotion
Medium Digital
Brief Personal work.

1

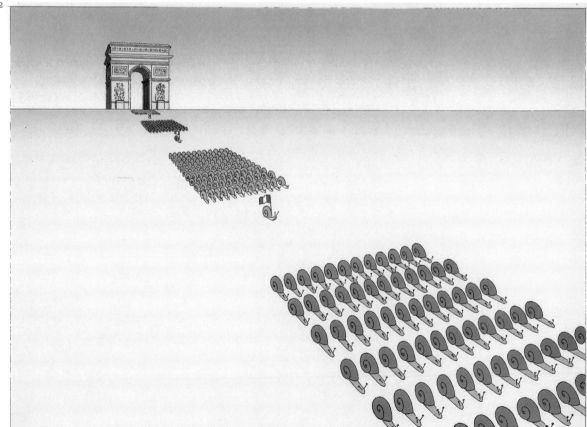

2

3

4

Ian Dodds

1. The Steep Approach To Garbadale

Section Editorial

Medium Digital

Brief Alban and Fielding wealthy cousins, are having a night out in Singapore in the early 1990's. The image needed to convey the vibrancy of the city.

Commissioned by Sarah Morley

Client Independent on Sunday

Guy Billout

2. French Elections

Section Editorial

Medium Watercolour and ink

Brief To capture the feeling that France is resistant to change.

Commissioned by Martin Colyer

Client Reader's Digest Magazine

Gillian Blease

3. S&P

Section Editorial

Medium Digital

Brief To accompany a chef's letter to the Agony Aunt in Restaurant Magazine: should he submit to his customers' requests for salt and pepper.

Commissioned by Joe McAllister

Client Restaurant Magazine

Hannah McVicar

4. The Garden

Section Self-promotion

Medium Linocut

Brief Gardening illustration.

1

Naomi Tipping

1. Here Are More Bullies

Section Books

Medium Digital collage

Brief Illustration from "Bully", a flap book that tackles the issue of bullying.

Commissioned by Sheri Safran

Client Tango Books

2. The Egg Factory

Section Books

Medium Digital collage

Brief Illustration from "Falcon's Fury", an adventure story with a moral message about battery farming.

Commissioned by Judith Escreet

Client Frances Lincoln

Bob Venables

3. The Gentlemen Profit Hunters

Section Advertising

Medium Oil

Brief To produce a example of 18th century Hunting scene featuring Sportsmen and hound for use in Bonhams Auction house Magazine.

Commissioned by Russell Wailes

Client RPM3

Commissioned for Artemis

2

Bish

1. Truth

Section Design

Medium Pencil,ink and digital

Brief To respond to a random word. I used words on skin to narrate a character without showing a face.

Commissioned by Sarah

Client Random House

2. Chess

Section Self-promotion

Medium Ink, pencil and digital

Brief To convey the emotion and tension of a chess game between two relative strangers.

Louise Weir

3. Uncle Arthur

Section Self-promotion

Medium Acrylic

Brief Produced as one of a series of "portraits I never did" for Illustrative exhibition.

Fossil Glanville

4. Locket ladies

Section Self-promotion

Medium Digital

Brief To promote a jewellery shop showcasing some of the products they sell.

3

4

2

3

Geoff Grandfield

1. Trouble Is My Business

Section Books

Medium Chalk pastel and Photoshop

Brief Illustrate the short story 'Trouble is my Business' by Raymond Chandler.

Commissioned by Joe Whitlock-Blundell

Client The Folio Society

2. Unusual Suspects

Section Editorial

Medium Chalk pastel and Photoshop

Brief In current state of fear of terrorism, everyone in the UK becomes a suspect.

Commissioned by Anne Rowe

Client The Times

Commissioned for The Times

Rebecca Bradley

3. My Family And Other Animals

Section Books

Medium Ink and acrylic

Brief Capture 1930's Greece, show family in kitchen chaos.

Commissioned by Sirida Pensri

Client Pearson

Ian Pollock

1. Penny Farthing

Section Self-promotion

Medium Ink

Brief Self promotion, ''Chariots of Ire''.

2. Marking Territory

Section Self-promotion

Medium Ink

Brief Self promotion, ''Chariots of Ire''.

3. Capitalism Hypocrisy

Section Editorial

Medium Ink, watercolour and gouache

Brief Editorial illustration for ''Last Word'' feature in Money Observer Magazine- 'capitalism's hypocrisy over ethos'.

1

2

Woking needs you!

Take the
carbon challenge!

11
tonnes of CO2
10
tonnes of CO2
9
tonnes of CO2
8
tonnes of CO2
7
tonnes of CO2
6
tonnes of CO2
5
tonnes of CO2
4
tonnes of CO2
3
tonnes of CO2
2
tonnes of CO2
1
tonne of CO2

3

4

Rod Hunt

1. Calor Village Of The Year 2016

Section Design

Medium Digital

Brief Project forward ten years to see what Calor Village of the Year Award might look like, with embedding sustainability in all aspects of village life.

Commissioned by Imogen Martineau

Client Forum For The Future

Commissioned for Calor Gas

2. Zombie Apocalypse

Section Self-promotion

Medium Digital

Brief The dead walk, & only characters from TV & film can save us from the zombie hoards. Name the films & TV programs!

3. Woking Needs You!

Section Design

Medium Digital

Brief Illustrate a 4800mm x 2000mm graphic lightbox about Woking's response to environmental issues. Selecting push buttons lights up & reveals facts/questions on specific activities.

Commissioned by Mike Hawkes

Client Real Studios Ltd

Commissioned for The Lightbox, Woking Museum & Gallery

4. Hero Of The Nation

Section Self-promotion

Medium Digital

Brief What if the Soviet Union had won the Space Race? Would Laika's desendants be exploring the stars? For a Space themed exhibition.

Commissioned by All Systems Go! Exhibition

Nathan Daniels

1. Company Cars

Section Editorial

Medium Digital

Brief Look after your drivers: how to safety and legally provide company cars for employees and ensure they use them legally.

Commissioned by Jodie Deakin

Client Haymarket Publishing

Commissioned for Management Today

2. Lloyds Keyboard

Section Editorial

Medium Digital

Brief How the London insurance market is updating its computer infrastructure.

Commissioned by Andrea Boughton

Client Beetroot Publishing

Commissioned for The Broker

3. Boardroom Duel

Section Editorial

Medium Digital

Brief Boardroom disputes and how to settle them.

Commissioned by Jane Moss

Client Director Publications

Commissioned for Director Magazine

Jan Bowman

4. Last Night Of The Proms

Section Editorial

Medium Digital

Brief Show curtain call on last night of Proms, including portraits of conductor and director.

Commissioned by Dav Ludford

Client BBC Music Magazine

Commissioned for BBC Magazines Bristol

5. Newington Green, Autumn

Section Design

Medium Digital

Brief Show this historic London square in autumn, incorporating a local landmark.

Commissioned by Nicky Southin

Client Newington Green Action Group

Commissioned for
Newington Green Action Group

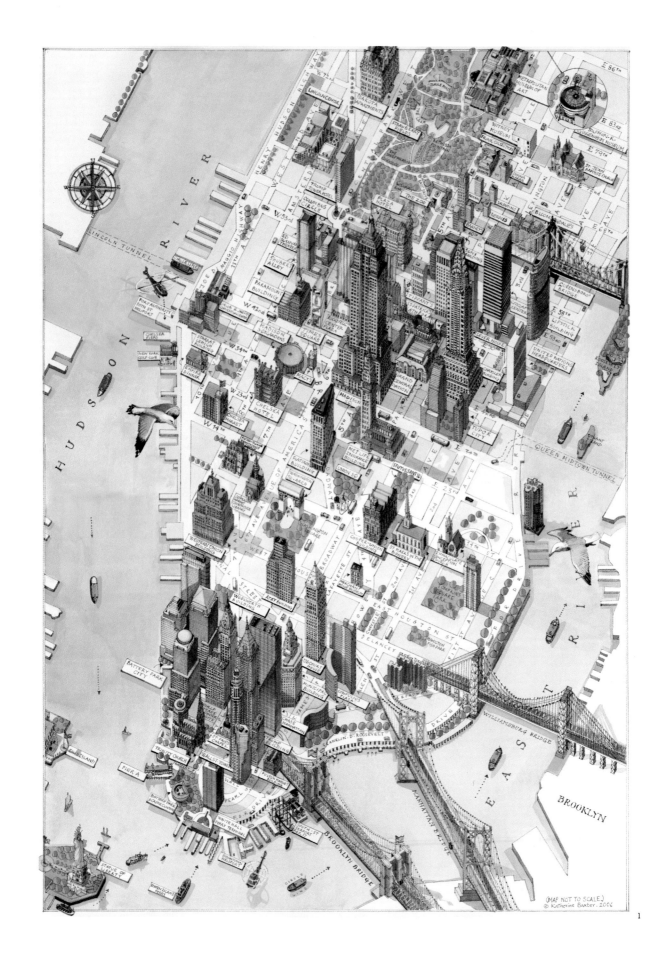

Katherine Baxter

1. New York

Section Editorial

Medium Watercolour and pen & ink

Brief Provide a full colour map with selected icons of Manhattan to be used as a poster.

Commissioned by Gruffyd Pryderi

Client Times Newspaper

Commissioned for Knowledge Supplement

Gerry Turley

2. Untitled

Section Self-promotion

Medium Digital and mixed media

Brief Image from development of a picture book idea.

Thomas Buchanan

3. Resolution 07

Section Self-promotion

Medium Mixed media collage

Brief Originally a commission for Men's Health to illustrate a new year's workout routine. The direction was to be in the style of the Russian Revolution, to accompany part one from the previous issue. I like the simplicity of this and the fact I was trying a similar regime.

2

Nancy Tolford

1. El Angelino	2. Beside the Sea
Section Self-promotion	**Section** Self-promotion
Medium Digital	**Medium** Digital
Brief Personal work inspired by a trip to Los Angeles.	**Brief** One of a series of works inspired by the English Seaside.

1

2

3

Nancy Tolford

1. Pueblo

Section Self-promotion

Medium Digital

Brief One of a series of works depicting different aspects of Spanish life and culture.

2. Motel on the Strip

Section Self-promotion

Medium Digital

Brief A piece based on the reminiscences of a woman who left home to live in Los Angeles in the 1940's.

Andrew Wheatley

3. White Rabbit

Section Self-promotion

Medium Collage

Brief Taken from a series of images I produced in response to Hunter S. Thompson's book 'Fear and Loathing in Las Vegas'.

3

4

A.Richard Allen

1. Beach

Section Self-promotion

Medium Pencil, acrylic and digital

Brief Self-promotional piece- a crowded seafront observed from a deck chair.

2. Taxidermy

Section Editorial

Medium Ink, acrylic and digital

Brief To accompany an article on paperless offices.

Commissioned by SooJin Buzelli

Client PLANSPONSOR Magazine

Lucia Gaggiotti

3. The Lion And The Mouse

Section Design

Medium Mixed media and digital

Brief Design of 3 boxes of children's biscuits range, based on Aesop's fables.

Commissioned by Julian Roberts at Irving Designs

Commissioned for Artisan Biscuits

4. The Owl And The Pussy-Cat

Section Design

Medium Mixed media and digital

Brief Design of 3 boxes of children's biscuits range, based on Aesop's fables.

Commissioned by Julian Roberts at Irving Designs

Commissioned for Artisan Biscuits

1

Lara Harwood

1. Notting Hill Carnival

Section Design

Medium Mixed media

Brief To create a colourful celebratory poster to advertise the Notting Hill Carnival event for posters on the London Underground.

Commissioned by Paul Crowley

Client Creator

Commissioned for Transport for London

2. Forensic Accounting

Section Design

Medium Mixed media

Brief To create a generic illustration on the subject of investigative accounting.

Commissioned by Lara Lockhart

Client BDO Stoy Hayward

3. Goats

Section Design

Medium Mixed media

Brief One of a series of five artworks commissioned for the delivery lorries of Booths Supermarkets.

Commissioned by Angelo Ferrara

Client Wolff Olins

Commissioned for Booths Supermarkets

2

3

"something old, something new," "something borrowed, something blue"

RiverCultures
FESTIVAL

3

Eleftheria Alexandri

1. In The Spirit of Tradition

Section Self-promotion

Medium Illustrator

Brief Ephemera, cheap editions, wood engravings, tradition, book illustration, fairy tales, Little Red Riding Hood.

Christine Hawthorn

2. River Cultures Festival

Section Editorial

Medium Pencil and digital media (Photoshop)

Brief To create an image representing the River Cultures Festival incorporating architecture around West India Quay, for use with articles on the website and promotional leaflets.

Commissioned by Rupert Breheny

Client mapped.tv

Andrew Baker

3. Back To The Future

Section Editorial

Medium Digital

Brief To promote Radio 4's 'The Archive Hour'. The programme: Back to the Future, dug into the BBC's archives to unearth outdated predictions for the future.

Commissioned by Ped Millichamp

Client BBC Worldwide Ltd

Commissioned for The Radio Times

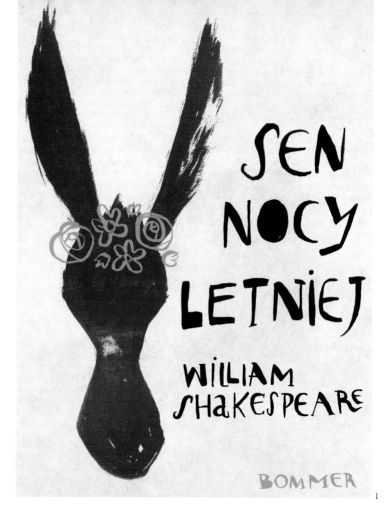

Paul Bommer

1. A Midsummer Night's Dream

Section Self-promotion

Medium Digital

Brief A personal experiment in technique and simplicity, inspired by Polish posters and a recent London performance.

2. Tourettes de France

Section Self-promotion

Medium Digital

Brief A self-promotional Bastille Day greeting card - a celebration of France, bicycles and word-play.

4

Max Ellis

3. Forever London

Section Advertising

Medium Digital

Brief Produce a Victorian engraved style image of a London scene for Spanish/US campaign.

Commissioned by Kate Mahon

Client Publicis

Commissioned for Beefeater Gin

4. Petshop

Section Advertising

Medium Digital

Brief Image part of the Lloyds 'Save The Change' campaign.

Commissioned by Hettie Rifkin

Client RKCR/Y&R

Commissioned for Lloyds TSB

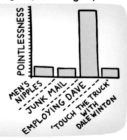

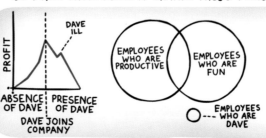

Stephen Collins

1. Paperclip Bastard

Section Editorial

Medium Digital

Brief Weekly cartoon for The Times, Career section.

Commissioned by Carol Lewis

Client The Times

Commissioned for The Times

2. Dave

Section Editorial

Medium Digital

Brief Weekly cartoon in the Times Career section.

Commissioned by Carol Lewis

Client The Times

Commissioned for The Times

3. Rock Legends Wallchart

Section Editorial

Medium Digital

Brief Newspaper-style wallchart about various rock legends, issued as a free gift with Q Magazine, May 2007.

Commissioned by Mark Taylor

Client Q

Commissioned for Q Magazine

3

Stephen Collins

Stephen Collins

1. Elaine's Lunch Break

Section Editorial

Medium Digital

Brief Cartoon for SoLondon magazine.

Commissioned by Juliet Howard

Client So London Magazine (now folded)

Commissioned for SoLondon Magazine

2. Will Self On Paris

Section Editorial

Medium Digital

Brief Feature by Will Self on enjoying the darker side of Paris.

Commissioned by Andrew Diprose

Client GQ

Commissioned for GQ

Lizzie Harper

3. Fire Salamander

Section Books

Medium Watercolour and gouache

Brief Illustrate fire salamander for identification purposes.

Commissioned by Amanda Bradbury

Client Wildfowl and Wetlands Trust

Commissioned for WWT Martin Mere

4. Grass-Anisantha Sterilis

Section Advertising

Medium Watercolour

Brief A4 image of the plant and flower of the grass Anisantha Sterilis for use in an advert for weedkiller (this grass being a weed to target) - one of 6 species illustrated.

Commissioned by Paul Townsend

Client MJL Advertising Ltd

Commissioned for Dow Agrochemicals - Indiana USA

3

Bill Sanderson

1. Accolades

Section Editorial

Medium Scraperboard and ink

Brief A Radio Drama: In 1973 A L Rowse's controversial publication of 'Shakespeare The Man', dared to suggest the true identity of the Dark Lady from Shakespeare's sonnets.

Commissioned by Hazel Brown

Client Radio Times

Commissioned for Radio Times

Naomi Ryder

2. Indian Summer

Section Design

Medium Freehand machine embroidery and hand stitch onto naturally dyed silk

Brief Create a colourful image for a summer music festival. Lively and sweet.

Commissioned by Rebecca Ashton

Client Firebrand Live

Commissioned for music festivals

Jasmine Chin

3. After A Long Day At
   The Office

Section Self-promotion

Medium Digital

Brief Santa plays host to his fellow collegues as they compare notes about those pesky children.

1

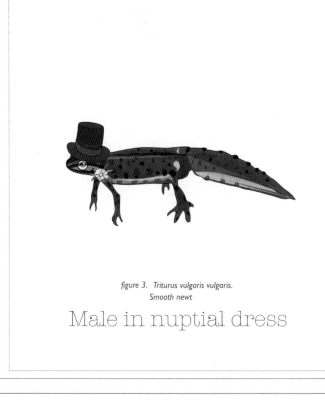

figure 3. *Triturus vulgaris vulgaris.*
Smooth newt

Male in nuptial dress

2

3

figure 5. *mustela erminea stabilis*

Stoat in winter dress

Tom Morgan - Jones

1. Lost Key... Lots Of Help!

Section Books

Medium Ink and digital

Brief 'Everyone looked for Charlie's key. They searched the floor, the lockers, the showers and everyone's boots and bags.' - illustrate.

Commissioned by John Harris

Client notreallybooks

Vicky Woodgate

3. Male In Nuptial Dress

Section Self-promotion

Medium Digital

Brief Part of a series of images for the Absurd Book of Wild Animals of the British Isles. A spoof of the 1950's Observers pocket books.

4. Stoat In Winter Dress

Section Self-promotion

Medium Digital

Brief Part of a series of images for the Absurd Book of Wild Animals of the British Isles. A spoof of the 1950's Observer pocket books.

Satoshi Kambayashi

1. Lost in Isolation

Section Editorial

Medium Digital

Brief New culture and language can take their toll when working in a foreign country, e.g. Japan.

Commissioned by John-Henry Barac

Client The Guardian

Commissioned for The Guardian (Office hours)

2. Road To The Fairy Tale Castle

Section Editorial

Medium Digital

Brief Scrutinising of the famous and the powerful is a necessary evil. In this case, Kate Middleton, when she was official girlfriend of Prince William.

Commissioned by Mike Topp

Client The Guardian

Commissioned for The Guardian

3. Rule Of The Foodies

Section Editorial

Medium Digital

Brief The rich are getting more obsessed with food, not less.

Commissioned by Gina Cross

Client The Guardian

1

2

Paquebot

4. Guilty As Charged

Section Self-promotion

Medium Digital

Brief Cat is caught red handed by the dog
while stealing a bird!

3

4

Jonathan Burton

1. Potter

Section Editorial

Medium Pen & Ink and digital

Brief Cover Illustration to accompany extracts from the Sebastian Faulks book 'Pistache'. The book parodies the writing style of Martin Amis and imagines him as if reluctantly sent to Hogwarts.

Client The Independent Arts Review

Commissioned for Independent Arts Review

2. Turner

Section Editorial

Medium
Assemblage, collage and photography

Brief To illustrate the media's reaction to the Turner Prize as a pastiche of Mark Wallinger's 'State Britain'.

Commissioned by Helen Whitley-Niland

Client GQ Magazine

3. Dr Freud Will See You Now Mr Hitler

Section Editorial

Medium Pen & ink (line and wash)

Brief A young, bed-wetting Adolf Hitler was referred to a newly opened children's psychiatric hospital in Vienna at the very same time that Dr Sigmund Freud was practising there.

Commissioned by Ped Millichamp

Client Radio Times

Commissioned for Radio Times

4. Roman Graffiti

Section Editorial

Medium Assemblage, collage, photography and digital

Brief Graffiti has been around since Roman times, it has recently been discovered. This article looked at this subject.

Commissioned by Martin Colyer

Client Reader's Digest Magazine

1

Chris Watson

1. Urban Scrawl

Section Books

Medium Ink drawing and digital colour

Brief Literary events booklet for London's "Spread the Word" organisation. Front and back cover as well as inside cameos illustrating theme of "Urban Scrawl".

Commissioned by Camilla Brueton

Client Spread The Word

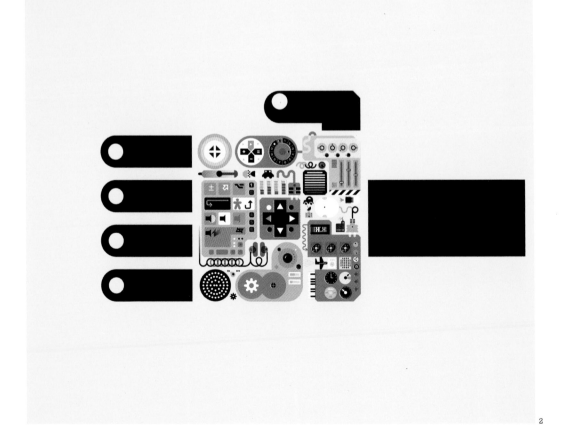

2

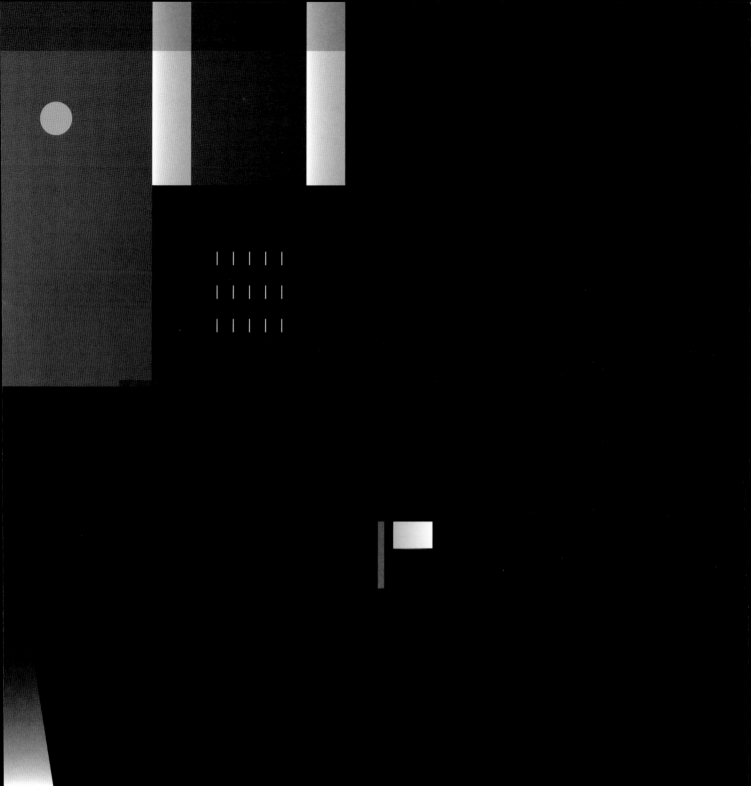

Peter Grundy

2. Technology At Your Fingertips

Section Advertising

Medium Digital

Brief Image for Vodafone campaign.

Commissioned by Mark Reddy

Client BBH

Commissioned for Vodafone

3. Battersea Power Station

Section Self-promotion

Medium Digital

Brief One of four images of a darker London for use in 'Grundini' the book. Downloadable from www.grundini.com.

1

2

5

3

4

David Humphries

1. Fire Engine

Section Self-promotion

Medium Digital

Brief To depict a visual oxymoron for a promotional mailout.

2. Binocular

Section Self-promotion

Medium Digital

Brief Part of a series of personal work about the great outdoors.

3. Trust Or Bust

Section Editorial

Medium Digital

Brief Glasgow museums and galleries are handing over their management to a charitable company.

Commissioned by Joe McAllister

Client Museums Journal

4. Quantum Reading

Section Editorial

Medium Digital

Brief Quantum reading makes mere speed reading look a bit like plodding, it takes to achieve extraordinary feats of speed and comprehension.

Commissioned by Graham Black

Client Financial Times

5. Where Have All The Uni Teachers Gone?

Section Editorial

Medium Digital

Brief Too many University courses, too few good teachers.

Commissioned by
Martin Colyer and Hugh Kyle

Client Reader's Digest Magazine

6. Red Tape

Section Editorial

Medium Digital

Brief Elected councillors are being gagged by over-zealous use of red tape.

Commissioned by
Martin Colyer and Hugh Kyle

Client Reader's Digest Magazine

6

1

Brigid Collins

1. The Scent Trail:
A Journey Of The Senses

Section Books

Medium Photographic montage

Brief For use on a hardback book cover,
showing the elements and ingredients in a
perfume made for the author who traces the
origins and the route of scent.
Photography by: bremnerphoto.co.uk

Commissioned by Claire Ward

Client Transworld

2. Down And Out
In London & Paris

Section Editorial

Medium Watercolour and collage

Brief To illustrate the radio broadcast.
Commissioned by Ped Millichamp

Client Radio Times

Frances Castle

3. Equasium Mailer

Section Advertising

Medium Digital

Brief To produce a lively, colourful image
to illustrate the title; "Every Child Needs a
Good Foundation to Build Upon" individual
elements from the image were used
seperately as stickers.

Commissioned by Brett O'Connor

Client Torre Lazur McCann

2

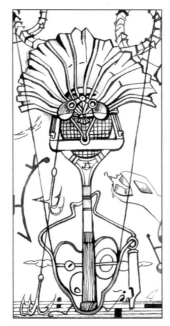

1

2

3

4

Lys Flowerday

1. Sports Et Divertissements
   After Erik Satie

Section Design

Medium Ink drawing

Brief Back drop design (reproduced large scale on canvas) for a performance featuring music and texts by Erik Satie.

Commissioned by Gilles Bourlet

Commissioned for
King of Hearts Centre for the Arts

Adrian B McMurchie

2. Reading Round Edinburgh

Section Books

Medium Watercolour and ink

Brief Front cover for children's book. Avoid creating the impression the book was written by JK Rowling (intro only) - lively, colourful, light, bit quirky not too much. literary/fantasy elements.

Client Floris Publishing

Fritha Lewin

3. Snog

Section Self-promotion

Medium Felt pen

Brief Seedy nights out in London.

Noma Bar

4. Naomi Campbell And The
   Human Rights Act

Section Editorial

Medium Digital

Brief To illustrate an article on the way the Human Rights Act is being used or abused especially in celebrity cases.

Commissioned by Martin Colyer

Client Reader's Digest Magazine

1

2

3

Graham Carter

1. Robot And Girl (Dusk)

Section Self-promotion

Medium Digital

Brief One in a series of works documenting the activities of a small boy and his various organic-looking, stunning mechanical devices, which he uses to help people or benefit his enviroment.

Emily Bolam

2. Buzzy's Balloon

Section Books

Medium Acrylic

Brief To illustrate "Buzzy's Balloon" written by Harriet Ziefert and published by Blue Apple Books.

Commissioned by Harriet Ziefert

Client Blue Apple Books

3. Does A Camel Cook?

Section Books

Medium Acrylic

Brief To illustrate "Does a Camel Cook?" written by Fred Ehrlich and published by Blue Apple Books.

Commissioned by Harriet Ziefert

Client Blue Apple Books

Ruth Hydes

1. Buxton Memorial Fountain

Section Self-promotion

Medium Gouache

Brief Illustration of the Buxton Memorial Fountain in the Victoria Tower Gardens, Westminster.

Client Unicef

2. Blackfriars Bridge London

Section Self-promotion

Medium Gouache

Brief Illustration of a London landmark, for a card from UNICEF for the UK corporate market.

3

4

Michelle Thompson

3. 22 Things

Section Editorial

Medium Digital.

Brief 22 Things to make the World a Better Place.

Commissioned by Cinders Mcleod

Client Globe & Mail

4. Untitled

Section Editorial

Medium Digital.

Brief To illustrate an article about a drug dealer.

Commissioned by Tim Fishlock

Client The Illustrated Ape

1

David McConochie

1. Child Development

Section Editorial

Medium Digital

Brief Illustrate an article tackling the subjective nature of child development and notions of individuality.

Commissioned by Rozelle Bentheim

Client Prospect

Commissioned for
Prospect Magazine May 2007

Tom Warne

2. The Claim

Section Self-promotion

Medium Acrylic paint and pencil

Brief To highlight the importance of medical insurance when travelling abroad.

3. Satisfaction

Section Self-promotion

Medium Acrylic paint

Brief Part of an ongoing project exploring different forms of personal escapism.

2

Paul Wearing

1. Tartines

Section Editorial

Medium Digital

Brief Full page illustration for recipe section in House & Garden, to include all six ingredients used in making crab tartines.

Commissioned by Fiona Hayes

Client Conde Nast

Commissioned for House and Garden

2. Silver & Bronze Vases

Section Self-promotion

Medium Digital

Brief Limited edition print for sale at charity auction in London.

Paul Thurlby

3. The Trouble With Beards

Section Self-promotion

Medium Digital

Brief To come up with a humourous image showing how beards can be irritating and unmanageable.

Alexander Beeching

4. A Mammoth Contemplates A Tree

Section Advertising

Medium Mixed media

Brief Create a A0 one-off print to adorn the Beechwood foyer.

Client Beechwood

Commissioned for Beechwood

1

2

3

4

1

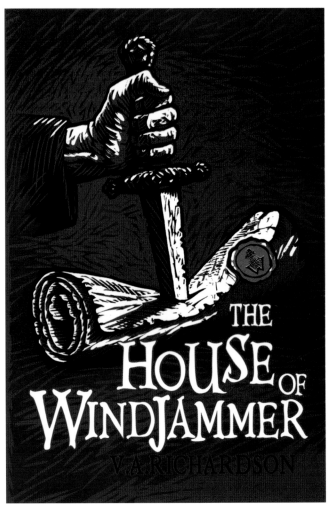

2

Lizzie Waterfield

1. Suffer And Bleed

Section Self-promotion

Medium Print and paper collage

Brief To illustrate instruction "Suffer and bleed". One of 10 from book entitled, "How to be a fairytale princess. For girls of an impressionable age".

David Bromley

2. House Of Windjammer Cover

Section Books

Medium Linocut and digital

Brief The book is an adventure story for children. Publishers wanted an image that looked as if it had been roughly hacked out of a piece of wood and printed badly.

Commissioned by John Fordham

Commissioned for Bloomsbury

3

4

Marcus Irwin

3. Hollywood Pin-up

Section Self-promotion

Medium Digital

Brief Promotional postcard adapted from personal print project, based on the faded glamour of the Hollywood movie star system.

Anna - Louise Felstead (MA)RCA

4. Junior Rates Galley, HMS Illustrious

Section Self-promotion

Medium Ink on paper

Brief I spent 6 days at sea on HMS ILLUSTRIOUS in May 2007 with a view to capturing the personal/personnel aspects of the ship. This galley drawing was one of many in order to celebrate the 25th anniversary of the ship.

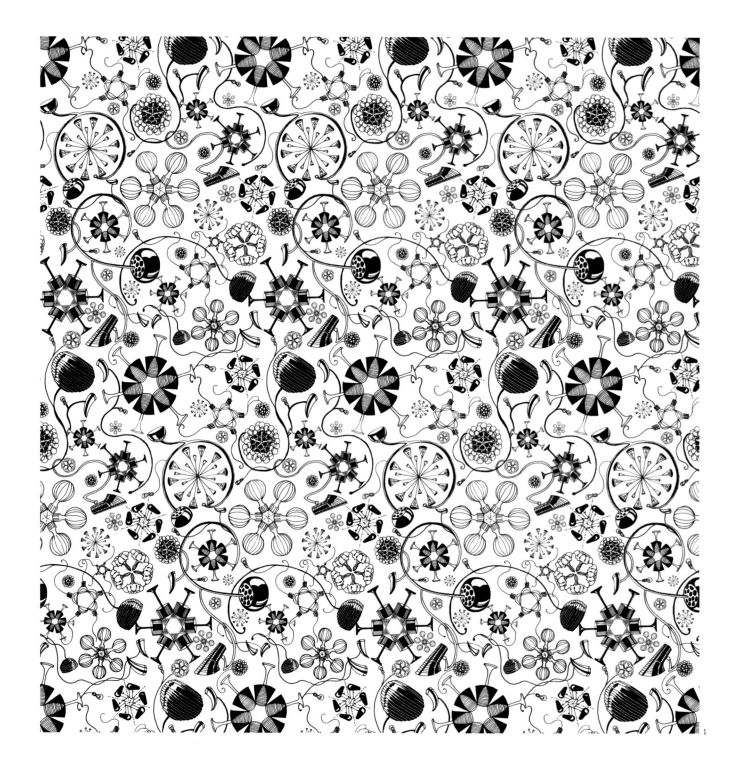

Daniela Jaglenka Terrazzini

1. Flos

Section Design

Medium Ink and digital

Brief To design a Christmas card that would unfold into a wrapping paper using the shapes of Flos' lights.

Commissioned by Mark Bonner

Client GBH

Commissioned for FLOS

2. The Old Man And The Sea

Section Self-promotion

Medium Charcoal

Brief To illustrate a book cover for The Old Man and the Sea by Ernest Hemingway.

3. Lady Chatterly's Lover

Section Editorial

Medium Mixed media

Brief To illustrate Lady Chatterley's Lover for a two part dramatisation on Radio 4.

Commissioned by Hazel Brown

Client Radio Times

Commissioned for Radio Times

2

3

Anna Ildiko Popescu

1. Ferdinand Fox And The
   Hedgehog

Section Self-promotion

Medium Graphite

Brief Illustration for a poem about a kind Fox
and a young Hedgehog.

2. Ferdinand Fox And The
   Hedgehog

Section Self-promotion

Medium Graphite

Brief Illustration for a poem about a kind Fox
and a young Hedgehog.

Laura Mullen

Triton, King Of The Sea

Section Self-promotion

Medium Pen & ink

Brief An illustration of Triton, the Ancient Greek God of the sea, who used a conch shell like a trumpet to control the ocean waves.

Lasse Skarbövik

1. Top 10 It

Section Editorial

Medium Digital

Brief
CA Magazine - 'Top ten tech issues 2007.'

Commissioned by Bernadette Gillen

Client CA Magazine

4

5

Jenny Simms

1. The Debutante

Section Self-promotion

Medium Digital collage

Brief A full page illustration for "The Debutante", a short story from "Wayward Girls and Wicked Women", edited by Angela Carter.

Joe Rogers

2. König Von Nichts

Section Self-promotion

Medium Mixed

Brief Open submission for Lamond Magazine; the brief was 'money'. The image depicts a man posing as someone who has money but infact has little.

3

4

Wendy Plovmand

3. Wealthy Walls

Section Design

Medium Aquarel, Photoshop, pen, pencil, collage and spraypaint

Brief WealthyWalls is a highly exclusive wallpaper design for people and places daring extreme wealthiness in everyday life. The title refers to the detailed illustration and the price while it encompasses reference to the decadence and overindulgence of high society living.

Commissioned by Trine Andersen

Client Wallcollection

Commissioned for Exclusive Wallpaper

Heather Gatley

4. Untitled

Section Design

Medium Mixed media and digital

Brief To produce an illustration of the front of the building where the company (Alfred E. Wenham) was situated for inclusion in a promotional brochure.

Commissioned by Andrew Cook

Client Metalhouse UK Ltd

Commissioned for Alfred E. Wenham

Katriona Chapman

1. Llama

Section Self-promotion

Medium Watercolour and pencils

Lucy Davey

2. The Delegates Choice

Section Books

Medium Mixed media

Brief To create a cover for the first book in the Mobile Library series in which a character gets lost in London with his mobile library.

Commissioned by Julian Humphries

Client HarperCollins

Commissioned for HarperCollins

Liz Toole

3. Jasper And Stone In Space

Section Advertising

Medium Acrylic

Brief Design a logo for a dog biscuit company, create two loveable dog characters to represent the company, placing them with the logo in an amusing space scene.

Commissioned by Adrian Stone

Client Jasper and Stone

Commissioned for Jasper and Stone

1

2

3

Allan Deas

1. Love For Sale

Section Self-promotion
Medium Mixed media
Brief Personal work.

2. Ships In The Night

Section Self-promotion
Medium Mixed media
Brief Personal work.

3. 5 A Day

Section Self-promotion
Medium Mixed media
Brief 'Eating 5 portions of fruit and
vegetables along with regular exercise is
very good for you'.

1

2

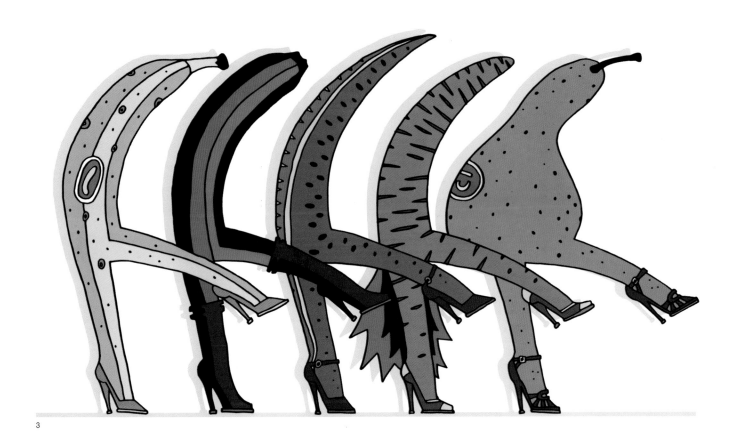

3

4

Dominic Trevett

4. Secrets Of The Digital Detectives

Section Editorial

Medium Pen & ink and digital

Brief Create an illustration that would show how fraud-detection systems combine dozens of clues to spot suspicious patterns in mountains of transactions.

Commissioned by Una Corrigan

Client The Economist

Commissioned for The Economist

1

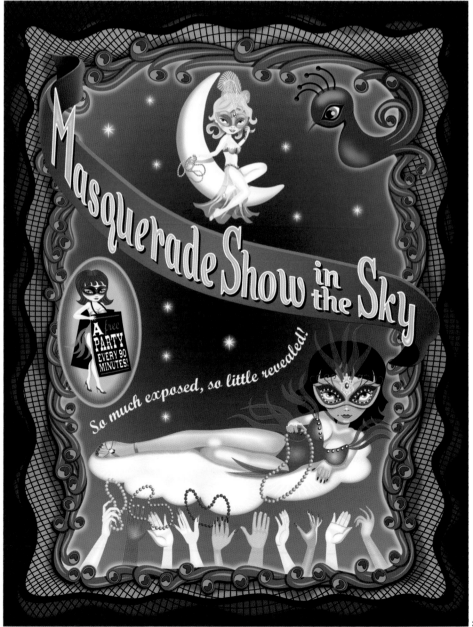

2

3

4

Sharon Tancredi

1. Save The Tiger

Section Editorial

Medium Digital

Brief To produce an image illustrating the rapidly depleting number of tigers in the wild and the fear for their extinction.

Commissioned by Ann Harvey

Client Pace Communications

Commissioned for Delta Sky Magazine

2. Masquerade Show In The Sky

Section Advertising

Medium Digital

Brief To promote cabaret show at Las Vegas hotel.

Commissioned by Carrie Evans

Client R&R Partners Advertising

Commissioned for RIO All-Suite Hotel & Casino Las Vegas

3. The Golden Goose

Section Books

Medium Digital

Brief Children's book of bed-time stories with a Buddhist theme.

Commissioned by Suzanne Tuhrim

Client Duncan Baird Publishers Ltd

Commissioned for Duncan Baird Publishers Ltd

4. New Age Tweety

Section Design

Medium Digital

Brief To create an image of Warner Brothers' "Tweety Bird" as a spiritual icon.

Commissioned by Brian Deputy

Client Warner Brothers Consumer Products Inc.

Commissioned for Warner Brothers Consumer Products Inc.

E133

Brilliant Blue FCF
FD&C Blue No.1
C.I. 42090

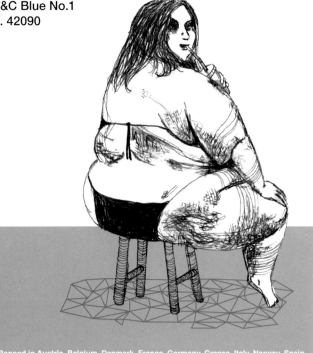

* Banned in Austria, Belgium, Denmark, France, Germany, Greece, Italy, Norway, Spain, Sweden, and Switzerland

1

2

Kat Stubbings

1. E133	2. Pub	3. Subway
Section Self-promotion	**Section** Self-promotion	**Section** Self-promotion
Medium Pencil and digital	**Medium** Pencil and digital	**Medium** Drawing and digital
Brief Self promotion	**Brief** Self promotional piece	**Brief** Self promotion

3

4

5

Modern Toss

1. Why Men Can't Manage Women

Section Editorial

Medium Mixed media

Brief Depict the masculine nature of many organisations and misunderstandings of the way women approach jobs, meaning many companies lose valuable female employees.

Commissioned by Sarah Habershon

Client The Guardian

Commissioned for Guardian: Work Section

Helen Wakefield

2. The Zone Of Faith Will Save Us From The Sovereignty Of The Mob

Section Editorial

Medium Mixed media

Brief Comment piece by Simon Jenkins on the role of taste in culture - the piece covers various issues including censorship.

Commissioned by Gina Cross

Client The Guardian

Commissioned for The Guardian: Comment and Debate

Jim Stoten

3. The Songs Remain The Same

Section Editorial

Medium Mixed media

Brief Cover illustration for Film and Music depicting the rise of the tribute bands and their fans.

Commissioned by Roger Browning

Client The Guardian

Commissioned for The Guardian: Film And Music

David Lyttleton

4. Can a Mere Nickname Help Our Hero Pack A Punch

Section Editorial

Medium Mixed media

Brief Regular columnist's illustration which appears weekly. Editorial illustration.

Commissioned by Barry Ainslie

Client The Guardian

Commissioned for The Guardian: Sport

Jo Ratcliffe

5. Why One Man Helped His Wife Die

Section Editorial

Medium Pencil

Brief Cover Story and inside feature depicting story of a man who helped his wife to die.

Commissioned by Richard Turley

Client The Guardian

Commissioned for Guardian: G2

1

2

Antony Cattini

1. Passenger

Section Self-promotion

Medium Photographic collage, watercolour, brown paper and Photoshop.

Brief One of a series of landscape illustrations portraying the incompatible relationships between the inhabitants.

Scott Chambers

2. Park Royal Studio Promotion

Section Advertising

Medium Mixed media

Brief To design an image for a T-shirt and poster to celebrate the 20th anniversary of Park Royal Studios, a film and photography studio.

Commissioned by Francois van de Langkruis

Client Park Royal Studios

3. Untitled

Section Editorial

Medium Mixed media

Brief To illustrate the diverse film festivals Australia has to offer in 2007.

Commissioned by Rebecca Burrell

Client The Sunday Telegraph

Commissioned for Sunday Magazine

4. Shazam

Section Self-promotion

Medium Mixed media

Brief Self-promotional piece.

fiota – low tar
2

1

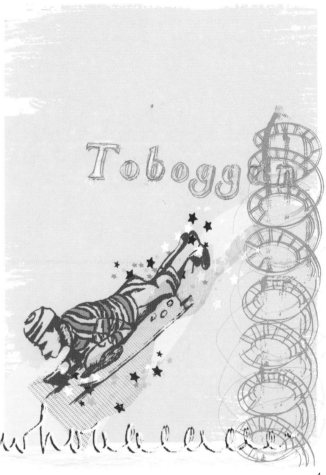

3

4

Jenny Rose

1. The Club Kids

Section Self-promotion

Medium Monoprint, airbrush and collage

Brief Designed for Gio-Goi, a brand that merges music, media and fashion, to portray their target audience - East-End cool kids as they leave the venue.

Lorna Siviter

2. No Ta To Low Tar

Section Self-promotion

Medium Digital

Brief 'Sorry sir this is a no smoking flight'... Haven't things moved on considerably!

3. Tiptoe Through...

Section Self-promotion

Medium Digital

Brief Tiptoe Through the Tulips...

4. Tobogganing (Whoaaaaa!)

Section Self-promotion

Medium Digital

Brief Tobogganing is so much fun... whoaaaaaa!

1

2

3

4

5

Andy Potts

1. NYC

Section Self-promotion

Medium Digital

Brief To create self initiated work for a joint exhibition in Hastings with Tim Marrs entitled 'Rebel Machines'.

2. Pier

Section Self-promotion

Medium Digital

Brief To create self initiated work for a joint exhibition in Hastings with Tim Marrs entitled 'Rebel Machines'.

3. IBM: CEO Bridge

Section Advertising

Medium Digital

Brief An illustration depicting IBM technology and asking how a company CEO sees his business strategy.

Commissioned by Victoria Azarian-Sabarese

Client Ogilvy Worldwide

Commissioned for IBM

4. The Twang: Wide Awake

Section Design

Medium Digital

Brief To design a cover for a song about the hangover and paranoia of the morning after.

Commissioned by Stephen Kennedy

Client FURY Design & Art Direction

Commissioned for Polydor Records

5. The Twang: Either Way

Section Design

Medium Digital

Brief To design a cover for a modern urban love song.

Commissioned by Stephen Kennedy

Client FURY Design & Art Direction

Commissioned for Polydor Records

2

1

3

Becca Thorne

1. When The Grass Turns Blue

Section Editorial

Medium Lino print

Brief To illustrate a song by Pete Leonard in an online magazine. To Include 1920/30's Blues influences and not conform to square frame, but to suit left to right scrolling.

Commissioned by Creature

Client Creature Mag

Lotte Oldfield

2. Sufficient

Section Books

Medium Mixed media

Brief One of the works commissioned to illustrate the ideas and methods of sustainable living in the book 'Sufficient' by Tom Petherick.

Commissioned by Emily Preece-Morrison

Client Pavilion Books

3. Sufficient

Section Books

Medium Mixed media

Brief One of the works commissioned to illustrate the ideas and methods of sustainable living in the book 'Sufficient' by Tom Petherick.

Commissioned by Emily Preece-Morrison

Client Pavilion Books

Serge Seidlitz

1. World Map

Section Advertising

Medium Hand drawn and digital

Brief Illustrate the world in seven days. Using different styles to make a collage of iconic imagery from around the world that forms the shapes of the continents.

Commissioned by Mark Reddy

Client BBH

2. Many Cultures One World

Section Advertising

Medium Digital

Brief Design an image that can be used for multi platform print (billboards, press ads etc) filled with iconic cultural elements from around the world.

3. KFC Hunger Strikes

Section Advertising

Medium Digital

Brief Create the visuals for an online computer game advertising the 'BIG DADDY BOX MEAL' special offer. Game objective: Stop hunger pangs traveling from the stomach to the brain by shooting them with strategically positioned KFC food weapons.

Commissioned by Nic Gorini

Client BBH

4

Jemma Robinson

4. Protest

Section Self-promotion

Medium Digital

Brief Protest against proposed runway expansions.

The flowers lift their
heads up to the sky
and smile at him

1

2

Fran Wardle

1. The Sunsetter

Section Self-promotion

Medium Screen printing pigment dyes

Brief A screen printed book titled
'The Sunsetter'.

Nick Radford

2. Pep Tree

Section Advertising

Medium Pen & ink and Illustrator

Brief Environmental awareness poster to
encourage sustainability within homes
and offices.

Commissioned by Matt Hocking

Client Leap Media

Commissioned for Leap Media

3. J.B.

Section Editorial

Medium Mixed media

Brief An article on James Brown, his life and
legacy following his death.

Commissioned by Helen Gilchrist

Client Stranger magazine

Commissioned for Stranger magazine

Stephanie von Reiswitz

1. Horsley's Sea

Section Editorial

Medium Ink on paper

Brief Illustrating a piece by Sebastian Horsley about his intense horror of and hatred for the sea.

Commissioned by Appleton, Bianchi, Bragg, Fox and Greene

Client Le Gun Magazine

Commissioned for Le Gun issue 3

Jay Taylor

2. Still Life

Section Self-promotion

Medium Mixed media

Brief Part of a self promotional book based on the idea of how illustration is not held in such high regard compared to fine art.

Tim Stevens

3. Tom Thumb

Section Self-promotion

Medium Pen & Ink

Brief He grew no bigger than a thumb; still his eyes were sharp and sparkling, and he soon showed himself to be a clever little fellow.

3

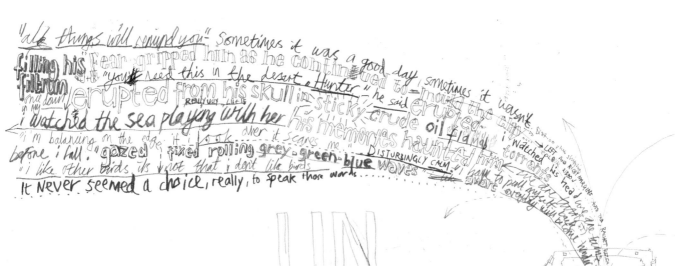

"all things will remind you" sometimes it was a good day, sometimes it wasn't
filling his fear gripped him as he continued to— march the city...
fillerton "you'll need this in the desert, Hunter" he said erupted
me down erupted from his skull in sticky crude oil I watched
REALLY WAY LIKE IS
i watched the sea playing with her his memories haunted him torrents
"i'm balancing on the edge. i look over it scares me
before i fall." gazed fixed rolling grey-green-blue waves" DISTURBINGLY CALM. I have to pull myself
"i like other birds, it's not that i don't like birds
It never seemed a choice, really, to speak those words..........

UN HEARD

1

MAKING THINGS
AT
MAKE

More
salmon
pink.

Z.

Rule(r)

scalpel.

1. CUT
2. SAW
3. STICK
4. Repeat.
but measure
first!

55 65

'Andrew' phoned
'Toni' at 11:30 After lunch
→5pm

MY MONITOR

R

2

David Sparshott

1. Unheard

Section Books

Medium Pencil

Brief An illustration for the cover of the book 'Unheard'; a collection of short stories by previously un-published authors.

Commissioned by Jonathon Ward

Client University of the West of England

2. Make People

Section Design

Medium Pencil

Brief A series of illustrations documenting the studios and those who work there of Make Architects in London.

Commissioned by Sophie Carter

Client Make Architects

3. Tea

Section Design

Medium Pencil

Brief To illustrate a guide of how to make the perfect cup of tea.

Commissioned by Nick Hand

Client Howies

Saeko Ozaki

4. Ecological Astology

Section Editorial

Medium Digital

Brief To illustrate 6 zodiacs as people, with characteristics of each sign in utopia of green environment, using recycling symbol as part of the elements.

Commissioned by Linda Burrows

Client News International Ltd

Commissioned for
The Sunday Times Style Magazine

1

2

Clare Shields

1. Numb

Section Self-promotion

Medium Photograpghy and digital

Brief The exploration of surreasim, human emotion and odd human behaviour through fashion, dance and textile print.

Cowface

2. Lord Of The Flies

Section Self-promotion

Medium Acrylic

Brief Proposed cover for William Golding's 'Lord of the Flies'.

3

ecm magazine & digital
awards 2007

friday september 21   to enter go to www.ecmawards.com
grosvenor house hotel
park lane   deadline for entries midday monday july 2nd
london w1

6pm-late

4

Sarah Perkins

3. Sophie's World

Section Books

Medium Mixed media

Brief A collage of the books main themes, the
universe, philosophy, religion etc - aimed at
an adult and juvenile market.

Commissioned by Charlotte Strick

Client Farrar, Straus and Giroux

Dan Smith

4. EMAP Ecm Awards Show 2007

Section Advertising

Medium Digital print

Brief A celebratory, upbeat illustration
that covers all markets served by EMAP
publications, to be used across various
collateral items like posters, event banners,
websites etc.

Commissioned by David Bostock

Client EMAP Consumer Media

DANIEL
EHRENHAFT

Harriet Russell

1. That's Life, Samara Brooks

Section Books

Medium Mixed media

Brief Cover for teenage fiction which suggests that science can be fun, with a large hand lettered title, and doodles and drips to give a lighthearted feel.

Commissioned by Marci Senders

Client Random House

Commissioned for
Random House Children's Books

2. Climate Chaos

Section Advertising

Medium Mixed media

Brief Ad to encourage people to pull together and act on climate change.

Commissioned by Joshua Blackburn

Client Provokateur

Commissioned for I Count

3

4

Matthew Hams

3. Winter Commute

Section Self-promotion

Medium Ink and Photoshop

Brief A self promotional piece based on the idea of commuting home from work in the Winter.

Teresa Murfin

4. Alan Thought He Was Being Funny

Section Advertising

Medium Digital

Brief One of a series of greetings cards for promotional use at Weight Wachers meetings and for sale online.

Commissioned by Alan Wood

Client Clemmow Hornby Inge

Commissioned for Advertising campaign

Jonathan Gibbs

1. A Tiger In The Sand

Section Books

Medium Wood engraving

Brief To illustrate the cover of Mark Cocker's book of selected writings on nature.

Commissioned by Anna Crone

Client Random House

Commissioned for 'Tiger in the Sand: Writings on Nature' by Mark Cocker

Terry Finnegan

2. Red Fire Dog

Section Design

Medium Watercolour

Brief Illustration to promote Chinese New Year in cafe/restaurant.

Commissioned by Gary Hogben

Client Cafe Blue

Commissioned for Chinese New Year Promo

4703

福春

1

2

3

Peter Mac

1. Tao On The Run In Outlaw China

Section Books

Medium Pencil and Adobe Illustrator

Brief Book cover for biography about a chinese artist who is on the run from the authority's in Tiananmen Square era China. He flees the country to Tibet where he becomes a master of sky burials. In this ancient tradition the bodies are fed to vultures and hence are taken away into the sky. He eventually fled from persecution to America where he is alive, well and a practicing artist. Gripping stuff!

Commissioned by Philip Gwyn Jones

Commissioned for Portobello Books

2. Coke At Work

Section Editorial

Medium Pencil and Adobe Illustrator

Brief Illustrate article about Drug use at work for magazine Druglink. The article suggests the use of cocaine in blue collar employement at work is on the increase.

Commissioned by Max Daly

Commissioned for Magazine Druglink

Dettmer Otto

3. Two States

Section Editorial

Medium Digital

Brief Is it possible for Israelis and Palaestinians to live together in one country?

Commissioned by Barbara Harper

Client The Guardian

Commissioned for Political Comment

4. Round Table

Section Editorial

Medium Digital

Brief A selection of distinguished 'elders' is to solve the world's problems.

Commissioned by Gary Cochran

Client The Saturday Telegraph Magazine

Commissioned for
The Saturday Telegraph Magazine

4

Jackie Parsons

1. Ausgang

Section Editorial

Medium Mixed media

Brief An illustration to accompany a short fiction piece about a young Jewish boy leaving pre-war Germany by boat in 1939.

Commissioned by Sarah Morley

Client Independent on Sunday

Commissioned for ABC magazine

Paul Bowman

2. God Did Not Sleep In Rwanda

Section Self-promotion

Medium Mixed media

Brief It was said that Rwanda was so beautiful that God slept there at night. This work is an attempt to make sense of the 1995 Rwandan genocide.

Christopher Gibbs

3. Harry Potter Stamp Packaging

Section Design

Medium Digital

Brief To design a presentation pack for the Harry Potter stamp series.

Commissioned by Ady Bibby

Client This is True North

Commissioned for The Royal Mail

Pete Brewster

4. Larynx

Section Editorial

Medium Digital scraperboard

Brief Illustrate finding your voice after surgery of the Larynx.

3

4

LAFF-O-MATIC

Ha ha ha
HA HA

Miles Cole

Comedy Machine

Section Editorial

Medium Photoshop

Brief Illustrate article celebrating and analysing the wealth and diversity of British comedy.

Commissioned by Alex Breuer

Client Esquire National Mags

Commissioned for Esquire Magazine

James Fryer

1. Dementia

Section Editorial

Medium Acrylic

Brief To illustrate an article about the degenerative brain disease dementia.

Commissioned by Gary Hyde

Client Saga Magazine

Commissioned for Saga Magazine

2. Big Brother

Section Editorial

Medium Acrylic

Brief The goverment is guilty of monitoring teachers far too much. As a consequence teachers are just not able to get on with their jobs freely.

Commissioned by Steve Place

Client News International

Commissioned for
The Times Educational Supplement Scotland

3. Enron

Section Editorial

Medium Acrylic

Brief The Enron scandal. How Enron lied to shareholders about the size and value of their company.

Commissioned by Giovanni De Mauro

Client Internazionale magazine (Italy)

Commissioned for
Internazionale magazine (Italy)

march

mon	tue	wed	thu	Fri	sat	sun
					1	2
3	4	5	6	7	8	9
10	11	12	13	14	15	16
17	18	19	20	21	22	23
24	25	26	27	28	29	30
31						

www.peopletree.co.uk

april

mon	tue	wed	thu	Fri	sat	sun
	1	2	3	4	5	6
7	8	9	10	11	12	13
14	15	16	17	18	19	20
21	22	23	24	25	26	27
28	29	30				

www.peopletree.co.uk

october

mon	tue	wed	thu	Fri	sat	sun
		1	2	3	4	5
6	7	8	9	10	11	12
13	14	15	16	17	18	19
20	21	22	23	24	25	26
27	28	29	30	31		

www.peopletree.co.uk

Chris Haughton

1. People Tree Calendar

Section Design

Medium Screen print

Brief Illustration / design for a handmade paper calendar made by a womens co-operative in Bangladesh. People Tree offer opportunities to disabled and disadvantaged artisans in the developing world.

Commissioned by Safia Minney

Client People Tree

Commissioned for People Tree

2. How To Turn

Section Editorial

Medium Digital

Brief Humorous piece about 'turning' ....'People who know exactly where they are going are rare and rather frightening. Life happens in a series of diversions'.

Commissioned by Maggie Murphy

Client The Guardian

Commissioned for Guardian Weekend Magazine

3. Butterflies

Section Self-promotion

Medium Digital

Brief Still for an unmade animation for Studio aka.

Commissioned by Grant Orchard

Client Studio aka

Ria Dastidar

4. Young London

Section Editorial

Medium Digital collage

Brief To create a cover illustration which captures contemporary 18-30 youth culture in London.

Commissioned by Tokunbo Ajasa-Oluwa

Client Catch - 22 Magazine CIC

2

Natasha Chambers

1. The Final Cherry

Section Self-promotion

Medium Illustrator and Photoshop

Kate Anderson

2. In Defence Of Eurovision

Section Editorial

Medium Pencil, pen and digital

Brief To design an image to illustrate the article 'In Defence of Eurovision' for the lifestyle section of The Skinny magazine.

Commissioned by Charlotte Rodenstedt

Client The Skinny

3

4

Nigel Coton

3. Noisy Britain

Section Self-promotion

Medium Mixed media

Brief To produce a self promotional illustration for an editorial article from the Guardian Newspaper about 'noisy Britain'.

4. You Don't Often See That...

Section Self-promotion

Medium Mixed media and computer

Brief Self promotional brief based on perspicacity and how people see things differently in life.

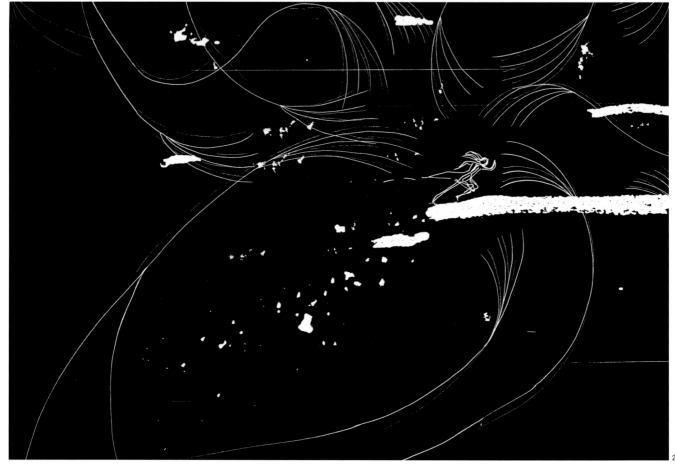

3

4

Rebecca Canavan

1. The Tain

Section Books

Medium Mixed media

Brief Cover artwork for Penguin Classics translation of ancient Irish tale about battles over a mythical bull. Depict bull as iconic figure: atmospheric, passionate, war colours.

Commissioned by Coralie Bickford-Smith

Client Penguin Books

Ami Clark

2. Silent / Desperation

Section Self-promotion

Medium Mixed media

Brief Experimental piece, conceptualising universal human emotions, expressed through use of narrative imagery.

Paul Boston

3. Three Men In A Float

Section Books

Medium Digital

Brief A funny journey in a milk float, an illustration which includes milk float, map of Britain, the two authors plus cameraman.

Commissioned by Sara Marafini

Client John Murray Publishers

Commissioned for Book cover

Chris Ede

4. Obsession

Section Self-promotion

Medium Pen, ink and Photoshop

Brief To create a series revealing my characteristics as an illustrator. This piece represents my obsession with writing down ideas wherever I am.

1

2

3

Jill Calder

1. USAville Girl

Section Self-promotion

Medium Ink and digital

Brief I decided to draw an iconic, bold female that also showed my hand lettering for a self promotion campaign in the USA.

2. Miss Julie

Section Design

Medium Biro and digital

Brief Image needed to promote "Miss Julie", a violent, sexually charged play being toured by the National Theatre of Scotland.

Commissioned by John Barbour

Client D8

Commissioned for NTS Ensemble

3. Tulips

Section Self-promotion

Medium Ink

Brief I wanted to create large scale, colourful, summery pullouts for my USA portfolios that featured people, plants and animals.

1

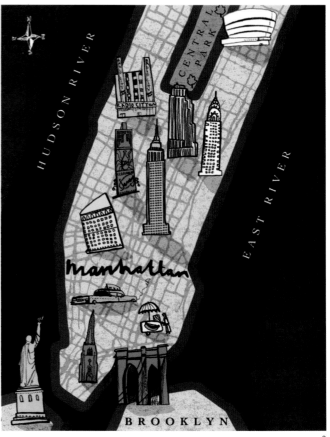

2

Jonathan Croft

1. Metropolis	2. Manhattan Map
Section Self-promotion	**Section** Self-promotion
Medium Digital	**Medium** Digital
Brief Produce a vibrant and detailed city image for a self-promotional postcard.	**Brief** Produce a simple map of New York City showing major landmarks.

Jonny Hannah

Complete Shakespeare
....

Section Editorial

Medium Digital collage

Brief Illustrate an article on a new edition of
the complete Shakespeare, incorporating the
complete list of plays.

Commissioned by Alex Macfadyen

Client the Sunday Telegraph

Commissioned for Books section

1

2

Terry Hand

1. Peace

Section Self-promotion

Medium Digital and mixed media

Brief An incongruous image to emphasise a point. An Indian chief, who strove for peace in his own time in a bleak, modern urban setting.

2. The Outsiders

Section Self-promotion

Medium Digital and mixed media

Brief Innocence and escape. The sense of being outsiders in an urban hinterland of motorway flyovers.

3

4

Gary Sawyer

3. Mexico City

Section Self-promotion

Medium Digital

Brief Promotional postcard image.

4. Celebration

Section Self-promotion

Medium Digital

Brief Promotional postcard image.

FIG. 905.—The principal motor pathways.

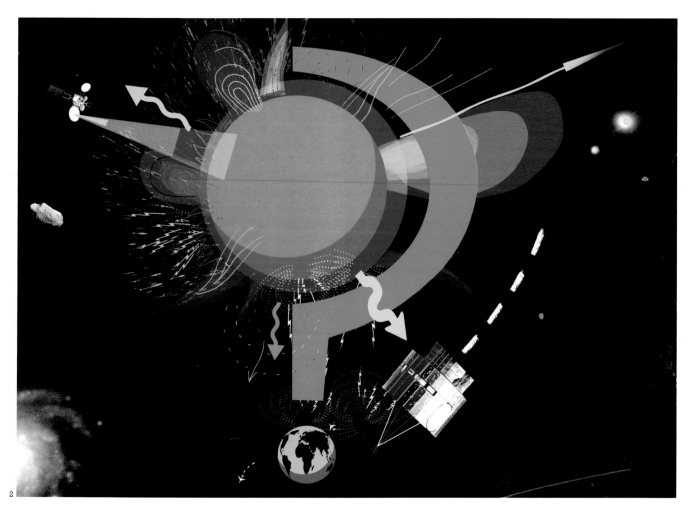

Frazer Hudson

1. Hearts And Minds

Section Editorial

Medium Digital

Brief Influencing the hearts and minds of a generation born into an era of 'war on terror'.

Commissioned by Gina Cross/Mike Topp

Client The Guardian

Commissioned for The Guardian

2. Space Weather

Section Editorial

Medium Digital

Brief The sun creates 'space weather' which has a major effect upon planet Earth's ecology and also interferes with systems operating within orbiting satellites and aircraft.

Commissioned by Alison Lawn

Client New Scientist

Commissioned for New Scientist

3. Hidden Depths Of Racism

Section Editorial

Medium Digital

Brief To what depths does Racism exist within our shores and how best we can we avoid racial conflict.

Commissioned by Gina Cross/Mike Topp

Client The Guardian

Commissioned for The Guardian

Wayward Water

Comb your hair

Comb is now negatively charged with electrons

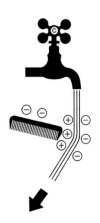

Hold the comb near a slow, thin flow of water from a tap.

The electrons in the comb attract positive charges in the water molecules, (and push away negative charges).

1

2

Frazer Hudson

1. Wayward Water

Section Books

Medium Digital

Brief Create a series of black and white line illustrations for youngsters to introduce and explain rudimentary scientific experiments they can practice at home. 'Wayward water' introduces them to the effect of negative and positive effect of electons.

Commissioned by Alison Lawn

Client New Scientist - book projects

Commissioned for
New scientist - book projects

Kevin Hauff

2. Orgasms

Section Editorial

Medium Digital and mixed media

Brief Illustrate the difference between the G Spot and Clitoral orgasm for the Times Body & Soul Newspaper section - keeping it subtle and amusing.

Commissioned by Anderida Hatch

Client The Times

Commissioned for Body & Soul Supplement

Peter Ra

3. Grant & Lee

Section Self-promotion

Medium Digital

Brief American Civil War Generals - Grant and Lee.

Jovan Djordjevic

1. Mince

Section Self-promotion

Medium Digital

Brief Fine Giclee Prints.

Nick Dewar

2. Carbon Offsetting: The Truth

Section Editorial

Medium Digital

Brief To illustrate a piece about whether carbon offsets really work.

Commissioned by
Martin Colyer and Hugh Kyle

Client Reader's Digest Magazine

1

2

3

4

Koichi Fujii

3. Rabbit Girl In The Woods

Section Self-promotion

Medium Adobe Illustrator

Brief Rabbit Girl ventures into the scary woods where unbeknown to her, evil monsters live. A scene from an adventure book for children.

John Charlesworth

4. Black Tie

Section Editorial

Medium Digital

Brief Illustration for Transmission Magazine Issue #07.

Commissioned by Jo Phillips Designer - Transmission

Client Transmission Magazine

Commissioned for Transmission Magazine

1

Gary Embury

1. Follow
....
Section Self-promotion

Medium Mixed media and digital

Brief Self promotion one of a series, inspired by 'Ghosts' a short story by Paul Auster.

2. Impulse Library Card Doodle
....
Section Self-promotion

Medium Mixed media and digital

Brief Commissioned by BBH for a press ad for Impulse. Illustration to be used on a library card background.

Commissioned by Rachel Leach

Client BBH

Commissioned for Impulse

Andrew MacGregor

3. Common
....
Section Editorial

Medium Pencils, paper, paint and pixels

Brief A Big Issue feature illustration on the Chicago based vocalist.

Commissioned by Sam Freeman

Client The Big Issue

Commissioned for The Big Issue

2

'Futuristic BoomBap!'

Graeme Neil Reid

1. 43 Years In The Third Form

Section Editorial

Medium Digital

Brief A nostalgic celebration of girls' comics from the 50s through to the 80s using escapism from the harsher realities of teenage life as a common theme.

Commissioned by Ped Millichamp

Client Radio Times

Commissioned for Radio Times

Steve May

2. The Great Ice Cream Con

Section Books

Medium Digital

Brief Front Cover of a Children's book.

Commissioned by Rachel Hickman

Client The Chicken House

Alex T Smith

3. I Hate Other People's Kids

Section Books

Medium Mixed media

Brief Cover for the book by Adrianne Frost.

Commissioned by Madeleine Meckiffe

Client Hodder & Stoughton

tick! tock! tick! tock!
tick! tock!
BONG!

3

4

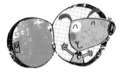

Super cool!

CLICK!

What a PICTURE!
FLASH!
SNAP!

see you later
ALLIGATOR!

1st

1st

faraway friends

4. Eliot Jones, Midnight Superhero

Section Books

Medium Mixed media

Brief Spread for the Children's book "Eliot Jones, Midnight Superhero".

Commissioned by Katherine Halligan

Client Scholastic Children's Books

5. Faraway Friends

Section Design

Medium Mixed media

Brief To design stationery and a poster for a penpal scheme between British and South African school children organised by Waitrose Foundation.

Commissioned by Susan Low

Client Waitrose

5

Simon Pemberton

1. Horror Classics

Section Books

Medium Mixed media

Brief Slip case for Horror Classics Trilogy
- asked to create a wrap around image
conveying a general air of menace rather
than relating to any specific story within.

Commissioned by Conorde Clark

Client Reader's Digest

Commissioned for
Reader's Digest Horror Classics

2. Propaganda War

Section Editorial

Medium Mixed media

Brief To depict the '' war of words''
Propaganda war that was the Spanish
Civil War.

Commissioned by Roger Browning

Client Guardian Newspapers

Commissioned for Guardian Review Cover

Chris Kasch

3. Radio Times Rock Of Ages Covers

Section Editorial

Medium Digital

Brief To create four change covers that illustrate and celebrate the television programme 'the seven ages of rock', that also works as one image.

Commissioned by Shem Law

Client Radio Times

Commissioned for Radio Times

Tim Marrs

4. Britain's Mr Crack Cocaine

Section Editorial

Medium Digital

Brief A real-life narrative of a police anti drugs unit.

Commissioned by Martin Colyer/Hugh Kyle

Client Reader's Digest Magazine

3

4

1

Peter Horridge

1. S.King Brand Pattern

Section Design

Medium Digital

Brief Produce an extensive decorative design influenced by Chinese laquer work, to be used as a branding device on fashion company packaging, carrier bags, print, etc.

Commissioned by Karin Soukup

Client TOKY Branding and Design

Commissioned for
TOKY Branding and Design

Tobias Hickey

2. Functional Depressive

Section Mixed media

Brief Women with successful professional careers and apparently happy lives are suffering from emotional and mental stress.

Commissioned by Baska Cunningham

Client You Magazine

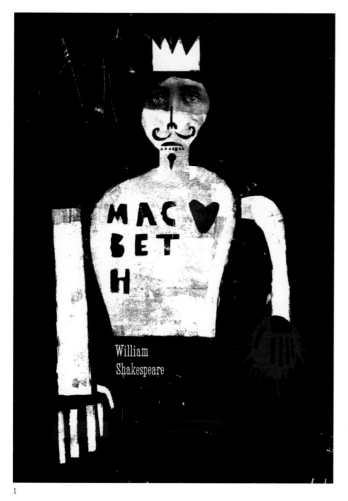

1

2

Ben Jones

1. Macbeth

Section Self-promotion

Medium Screen print and digital

Brief Proposed promotional theatre poster for a season of Shakespeare plays.

Matthew Johnson

2. Noam Chomsky

Section Self-promotion

Medium Mixed media

Brief Portrait of author and political activist Noam Chomsky.

Paul Garland

3. Moulin Rouge, Paris

Section Self-promotion

Medium Mixed media

Brief To provide a 21st Century Poster image for the Burlesque Parisian show.

MOULIN ROUGE

PARIS

1

2

3

4

Alexandra Lazar

1. Visceral Is An Animal

Section Editorial

Medium Ink and digital

Brief The brief was to depict dual erotic/ antagonistic confrontations for Chroma (queer literary and arts journal).

Commissioned by Shaun Levin

Client Chroma

Jacquie O'Neill

2. La Vida Loca

Section Editorial

Medium Digital

Brief Woman sat in a chair looking out of the window, seeing a man walking past. To illustrate that there are plenty more 'fish in the sea!'.

Commissioned by Kourtney McKay

Client Associated Publications Inc

Commissioned for La Vida Loca Editorial

Alan Heighton

3. Wolfie Darts

Section Editorial

Medium Digital

Brief Produced for Simon Hattenstone sports column about the 2007 darts final and the focus on 'Dart WAGS'.

Commissioned by Barry Ainslie

Client The Guardian

Commissioned for Sports Column

Steve King

4. Famous Faces, Strange Places

Section Self-promotion

Medium Acrylic

Brief One of a number of images displayed in exhibition of famous figures placed in unusual local surroundings.

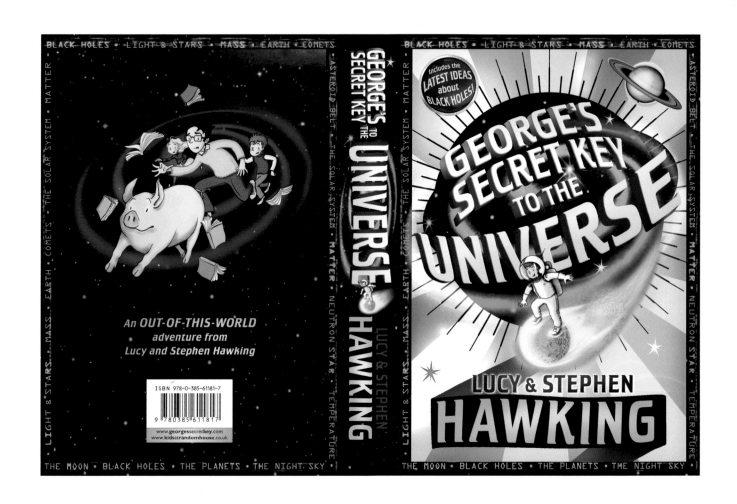

Garry Parsons

George's Secret Key To
The Universe

Section Books

Medium Digital

Brief Book jacket including all the main
characters for a gripping new space
adventure from Lucy and Stephen Hawking.

Commissioned by James Fraser

Client Random House Children's Books

Commissioned for Doubleday

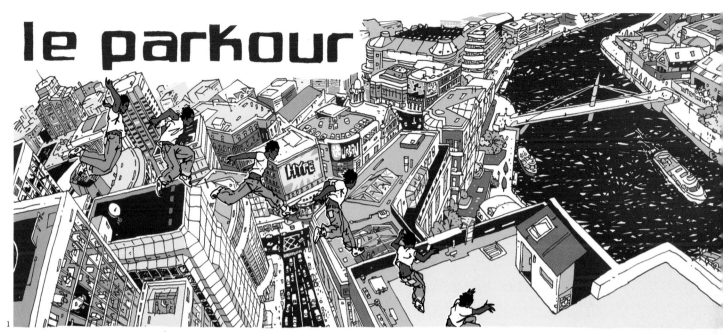

le parKour

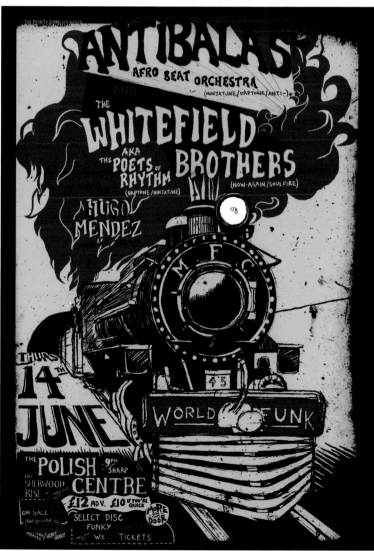

Dylan Gibson

1. Parkour

Section Advertising

Medium Ink and Photoshop

Brief To create a dynamic image that captures the spirit of the sport of Parkour in an urban setting.

Lewis Heriz

2. Antibalas and The Whitefield Brothers

Section Design

Medium Pencil, pen & ink and Photoshop

Brief Produce a dramatic poster representing the music of raw 60s Funk, Afrorock, Psych and Tropical rhythms to promote The Mighty's summer double bill.

Commissioned by Hexford

Client The Mighty Funk Collective

Emma Harding

1. Step-Parenting: The Highs And Lows

Section Editorial

Medium Biro, collage and digital

Brief Readers Family Forum - Step Parenting.

Commissioned by Sarah Habershon

Client The Guardian

Commissioned for
Family section - Family Forum

Swava Harasymowicz

2. Putting Daisy Down

Section Editorial

Medium Mixed media

Brief To illustrate a short story by Jay McInerney about a power struggle within a married couple.

Client The Guardian

Matthew Richardson

3. Adverbs

Section Books

Medium Mixed media and digital

Brief Cover for 'Adverbs' by Daniel Handler. Set in San Francisco, 'Adverbs' are a series of inter-related stories about different forms of love.

Commissioned by Richard Bravery

Client HarperCollins Publishers

Commissioned for HarperCollins

3

1

2

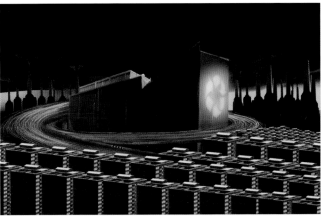

3

Clare Mallison

1. Trattoria Da Aldo

Section Editorial

Medium
Felt tips, pen & ink and digital media

Brief A drawing of the interior of my
favourite restaurant.

Commissioned by Paula Yacomuzzi

Client The Creator Studio

Commissioned for The Creator Studio

Sarah Gooch

2. Alternative Transport

Section Editorial

Medium
Collage, painting, line drawing and digital

Brief To play with the theme of 'alternative
transport' in a fun, imaginative way to
produce an original piece of artwork.

Commissioned by Dale Donley

Client Aesthetica Magazine

Commissioned for Aesthetica Magazine

Matt Murphy

3. The Genie In The Bottle

Section Books

Medium Collage

Brief Provide illustrations to accompany the
story of a child and his grandfathers journey
following a planets demise at the hands of
climate change.
Appeal to children aged 9 – 16.

Commissioned by
Hugh Montgomery/Monica Bratt

Client Pagewise

3

Philip Hurst

1. Maybe Not Cat

Section Self-promotion

Medium Watercolour

Brief Unpublished children's picture book.

Henning Löhlein

2. Take Over

Section Editorial

Medium Acrylic

Brief Smaller bookshops are getting taken over by larger book chains.

Commissioned by Dr. Torsten Casimir

Client Börsenblatt

Sarah Jane Preston-Bloor

3. Oscar And The Moon

Section Self-promotion

Medium Acrylic paint

Brief A picture book idea where Oscar has ran out of milk so he decides to visit the moon which is made of swirling milk.

Chris Garbutt

1. Zoobus

Section Self-promotion

Medium Digital

Brief For a full page advertisement to showcase various animal characters and hand rendered type.

Naomi Manning

2. Heads, Hands and Birds

Section Self-promotion

Medium Acrylic and ink

Brief To take a title from a popular painting and produce an LP cover from the same name.

3

4

Elisa González (Elita)

3. Grand Corps

Section Self-promotion

Medium Computer assisted illustration

Brief Illustrate an elephant over the words Grand Corps; It should be eye-catching but not as important as the type work.

John Holcroft

4. Pizza Menus

Section Self-promotion

Medium Digital

Brief My own version of the Pizza Express Menu Covers. I have based my designs around the 'create your own' concept.

Harvey

1. Ship In A Bottle

Section Self-promotion

Medium Print and digital

Brief Originally produced for self-promotion, but was later used as part of an online 'poster' for the band 'Mt.' and Motive Sounds Recordings.

Mel Croft

2. Bordeaux Map

Section Books

Medium Mixed media

Brief One of a series of regional maps of France to illustrate the book 'Oz and James's Big Wine Adventure'.

Commissioned by Eleanor Maxfield

Client BBC Worldwide Ltd

Commissioned for
Oz and James's Big Wine Adventure

3

4

Gun Dog.

Pointer.

Springer

After Dinner Speech.

4

Kid Dalek.

5

Clinton Banbury

1. Gun Dog

Section Self-promotion

Medium Ink and watercolour

Brief Illustration for humorous dog training manual, matching breed or dog type with a memorable image.

2. Pointer

Section Self-promotion

Medium Ink and watercolour

Brief Illustration for humorous dog training manual, matching breed or dog type with memorable image.

3. Springer

Section Self-promotion

Medium Ink and watercolour

Brief Illustration for humorous dog training manual, matching breed or dog type with memorable image.

4. After Dinner Speech

Section Self-promotion

Medium Ink and watercolour

Brief One of a series of animal inspired humorous illustrations relating to real life situations.

5. Kid Dalek

Section Self-promotion

Medium Ink and watercolour

Brief One of a series of humorous illustrations for editorial on the way children are affected by TV programs.

Tyrannosaurus Regina.

Clinton Banbury

Tyrannosaurus Regina

Section Self-promotion

Medium Ink and watercolour

Brief Illustrating a series of humorous
alternative dinosaur types.

Jamie Sneddon

Pwnage!

Section Editorial

Medium
Freehand MX, SketchUp Pro and Photoshop

Brief Official PSP [gaming] magazine.
Haloween feature. Full DPS. ''Why we like
being scared''. Player(s)/characters in total
safety, 'owning' a room full of the undead.

Commissioned by Ian Dean

Client Future Publishing

Commissioned for
Official PSP Guidebook [gaming publication]

Images 32   page 223

New Talent

Works by full-time students, including those who graduated in 2007.

Richard Keenan

Sarah Pascoe

Andrew Coningsby

Yuko Shimizu

Matthew Shapland

Judges

Andrew Coningsby, Managing Director, Début Art Illustration Agency

Andrew Coningsby founded the illustration agency Début Art in 1985 and in 1994 established the contemporary illustration specialist gallery The Coningsby Gallery. Both concerns continue to develop apace. In 2006 Andrew was delighted to accept an invitation to join the Association of Illustrators Council and the Pro-Action: Illustration Campaign and Liaison Group. Andrew is a passionate and well informed advocate of illustrators commercial and artistic interests.

"I thought the quantity and quality of entries to the Students Category was high this year with many submissions demonstrating an original style and approach as well as technical skill. Above all I was impressed by the original 'takes' that many of these younger wannabe illustrators had in response to the briefs they had been given."

Richard Keenan, Art Editor, Time Out Magazine

Richard has been commissioning illustration at Time Out for six years, working with many illustrators with a diverse range of styles, from small weekly series to covers.

"The quality of Student submissions was high with some outstanding entries. The many hand-drawn illustrations - and one 3D pop-up - shows a strong sense of craft this year, with close attention being paid to the details: the line, pencil, the ink, the surface."

Comments on winning images:
Gold: 'Rapunzel': Beautifully crafted and executed illustration. The intricate and ornate balance perfectly with the sparse, the subject matter evocative, melancholic. Very sophisticated.
Silver: 'Cradle To Grave Cards': Fantastic in ambition and scale. The combination of typography and portrait in colour and style is brilliant. Just beautifully done. I would love to see this collection printed commercially.
Bronze: 'Lucy Goes To Market': Lovely warm tones fit the subject matter absolutely. The drawing and spare use of colour is expertly achieved. I could imagine the adventures of this girl filling a whole book.

Sarah Pascoe, Head of Art Buying, BBH

Sarah started working at JWT in 1986 in the Art Buying department, since then she considers herself incredibly lucky to have worked with some of the most creative people in the world of advertising and beyond, who in turn have made it very easy for her to stay passionate about the job that she does.

"I was encouraged with the wealth of talent emerging from the colleges and look forward to working with them in the future."

Matthew Shapland, Creative, Red Bee Media

Matthew currently writes and directs as a creative for Red Bee Media. CBeebies and CBBC feature many of his on air campaigns which include live action and animation sequences.

"It's good to see young illustrators communicate with wit and ability."

Yuko Shimizu, Illustrator, New York

Yuko Shimizu went back to study illustration at the School of Visual Arts after working in corporate Japan for more than 10 years. She received an MFA from the School of Visual Arts (SVA) in 2003 and she has been working as a freelance illustrator as well as instructor at SVA. Clients include: Microsoft, Pepsi, Nike, MTV, Warner Music, Time, The New York Times, etc.

"It was so much fun and interesting to see what is going on in art schools in England. I was surprised by the high quality of work. I had a few I felt like they are a really high professional level. Very exciting."

Comments on winning images:
Gold: Fantastic composition and great sense of limited color palette. There is a lot of mystery in the image which captures the viewer.
Silver: So much fun. Makes me want to keep looking at each panel to find out the story. Good graphic design as well as great illustration.

Gold

Nick Mott

Rapunzel

College University College Falmouth

Medium Pencil, photocopy collage and digital

Brief To produce a series of images to illustrate the Grimms fairytale 'Rapunzel'.

Course Leader Alan Male

Course BA (Hons) Illustration

Nick Mott graduated from University College Falmouth's Illustration BA course with a first class honours degree in June 2007. Since then he has been starting to work as a commercial illustrator producing illustrations for the Guardian Weekend magazine. This image illustrates the Brothers Grimm story 'Rapunzel'. The image is one of a series of four. The illustrations were produced with an adult audience in mind to be included in a compendium of folk tales.

The illustrations are constructed manually using a combination of black pencil and manipulated photocopy collage. Only when the images have been put together using scissors, glue and pencil, are they then minimally altered digitally - the digital process only allowing for a subtle change of colour here and there.

Nick starts with a very rough thumbnail idea then quickly starts to construct a background or landscape. This background is usually photocopied several times to allow some experimentation of where to place subsequent elements of the illustration. The process tends to be quite organically improvised while sticking within a compositional idea. Several ideas are tried but it is obvious when something is 'correct'. The main aim of these images was to convey as much melancholy, tension, loneliness, strangeness and dark beauty as is contained within the fairy tale.

Nick tries not to be influenced by contemporary illustration preferring his love of traditional etching and drawing and surrealist fine art to subtly enrich his images. Nick sees the 'unfashionable' quality of his illustration to be one of its strengths. Nick also tries to be as original and idiosyncratic as possible, with a view to ensuring that his illustration looks different to anything else currently being produced by others.

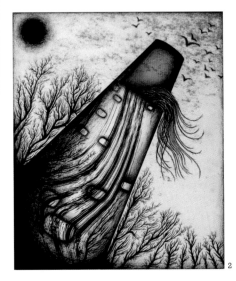

1

2

1 Roughs

2 Visuals

3 Winning illustration

1

2

Silver

Haruka Shinji

From The Cradle To The Grave
Collector's Cards

College Kingston University

Medium Pen and computer

Brief One of the drawings of a personal project called "From the Cradle to the Grave".

Course Leader Geoff Grandfield

Course Illustration and Animation

Shinji was born in Japan, but spent most of her time in South Korea and China. She arrived in Kent for her foundation course in art and design. After struggling in Kent, she moved to Kingston for her degree course in Illustration and Animation where she explored her interests including old maps, specimens (and their owners' obsession), insects, stuffed animals, railways, unattended stations, the circus and anatomy. She is obsessed with screenprinting and enjoys getting her hands dirty. In her illustrations, she loves mingling real stories into her imaginary world. She currently studies Communication Art and Design at the Royal College of Art in London and continues to get her hands dirty.

1 Winning illustration

2 Sketches

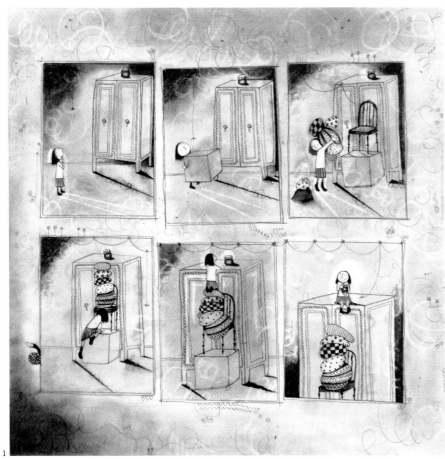

Bronze

Imogen Clare

Lucy Goes To Market

College University of Northampton

Medium Pencil

Brief A student project to produce a children's book. I collaborated with my mother, a writer, and illustrated an alphabet book about a little girl called Lucy, who visits a mythical marketplace and collects rare and unusual delights.

Course Leader John Holt

Course BA (Hons) Illustration

After completing her A levels in 2003 Imogen took a gap year and pursued her love affair with Africa by living in Ghana, where she painted murals on walls and tigers on faces. She began to study English Literature at the University of Sussex where she consumed more children's books than adult novels. Following a Foundation course in Art and Design, Imogen began a degree in Illustration in 2005. 'Lucy Goes To Market' won first prize in the Macmillan Prize for Children's Picture Book Illustration 2007. The ideas and drawings had to be detailed, fantastical, imaginative and quirky and had to contain a strong narrative sense. It has been a precious and exceptional few years, where the space to explore and experiment has enabled her to grow in confidence and find a personal voice.

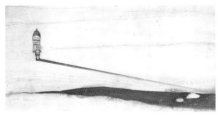

1 Winning illustration

2 Sketches

Ants scurrying in all directions
with purpose but no meaning.
Lost in a dried-up sea of hot air,
struggling to breathe.
Metallic clash of cogs, teeth not giving,
stopping to squeal.
Angry swarm nose-dives out,
minding the gap.
Frantic tunnelling upwards
towards a promised light.
But no pearly gates,
no saints.
Corporate walls, corporate faces,
flushed out into the abyss.

Jade Angus

My Interpretation London Vs Brighton

College Northumbria University at Newcastle

Medium Pen and ink

Brief My brief was to create a piece of artwork that was an expression of a place that I'd visited. I chose to use London Vs Brighton as I felt strongly about both places. My illustrations show how different the places appear, I reinforced my feelings with poems.

Course Leader Ted Carden

Course BA(Hons) Graphic Design

Erica Dorn

1. Tamika And Tiger Head For Home

College London College of Communication

Medium Mixed media

Brief A spread from a children's book project in collaboration with writer Margaret Ousby. The story, entitled "Are We There Yet?" is about a little girl's adventure through a series of extraordinary "worlds".

Course Leader Paul Bowman

2. Into The Tunnel

College London College of Communication

Medium Mixed media

Brief A spread from a children's book project in collaboration with writer Margaret Ousby. The story, entitled "Are We There Yet?" is about a little girl's adventure through a series of extraordinary "worlds".

Course Leader Paul Bowman

3. Belt Motel

College London College of Communication

Medium Photography and collage

Brief Design a cover for the blues/folk/experimental band, Belt Motel. The image should refer to the grainy, smoky quality of the music.

Course Leader Paul Bowman

Sara Feio

4. Cat Fur

College London College of Communication

Medium Cut-out, ink and digital

Brief (Vent) Defending what I believe in. I chose to vent on animal cruelty and raise awareness to the usage of cat and dog's fur by clothing companies.

Course Leader Paul Bowman

3

4

Martyn Warren

1. Why The Nazis Lost	2. Why The Nazis Lost
College Southampton Solent University	**College** Southampton Solent University
Medium Mixed media	**Medium** Mixed media
Brief One of 10 self-promotional postcards from the set 'Why The Nazis Lost'.	**Brief** One of 10 self-promotional postcards from the set 'Why The Nazis Lost'
Course Leader Derek Rogers	**Course Leader** Derek Rogers
Course MA(Hons) Illustration	**Course** MA(Hons) Illustration

the allies had nature on their side.

2

3

"AN ASTONISHING DEBUT.... FIGHT CLUB IS A DARK, UNSETTLING, AND NERVE-CHAFING SATIRE". THE SEATTLE TIMES

Chuck Palahniuk's darkly funny first novel tells the story of a disenfranchised young man frustrated with his bureacratic job and superficial relationships and disillusioned with the consumer culture's prepackaged pleasures. Relief for him and his peers comes in the form of Tyler Durden, the intensely charismatic inventor of Fight Club. Waiters, clerks, and middlemen seek out the visceral satisfaction of secret after-hours boxing matches in the basements of bars, thinking they have found a way to live beyond their confining and stultifying lives. But in Tyler's world there are no rules, no limits, no brakes.

"Fight Club offers diabolically sharp and funny writing". — THE WASHINGTON POST BOOK WORLD

"A powerful, dark, original novel... A memorable debut by an important writer". ROBERT STONE

Fight Club

Chuck Palahniuk

Fight Club

Chuck Palahniuk

Emily Paget

3. Fight Club

College Middlesex Universsity

Medium Collage and digital

Brief To illustrate the book by Chuck Palahniuk.

Course Leader Andrew Baker and Nancy Slonims

Course BA(Hons) Illustration

2

3

Katrina Hansford

1. The Rose Garden

College Southampton Solent University

Medium Watercolour, pen and ink

Brief One of a series of images produced to illustrate MR James' 'Selected Ghost Stories'.

Course Leader Derek Rodgers

Course BA(Hons) Illustration

2. Willow

College Southampton Solent University

Medium Pen and ink

Brief Produced for my own satisfaction as a record of our growing, mischievious puppy, Willow.

Course Leader Derek Rodgers

Course BA(Hons) Illustration

3. Suppertime

College Southampton Solent University

Medium Pen and ink

Brief Produced for my own satisfaction from sketches and photographs of a friend's cat.

Course Leader Derek Rodgers

Course BA(Hons) Illustration

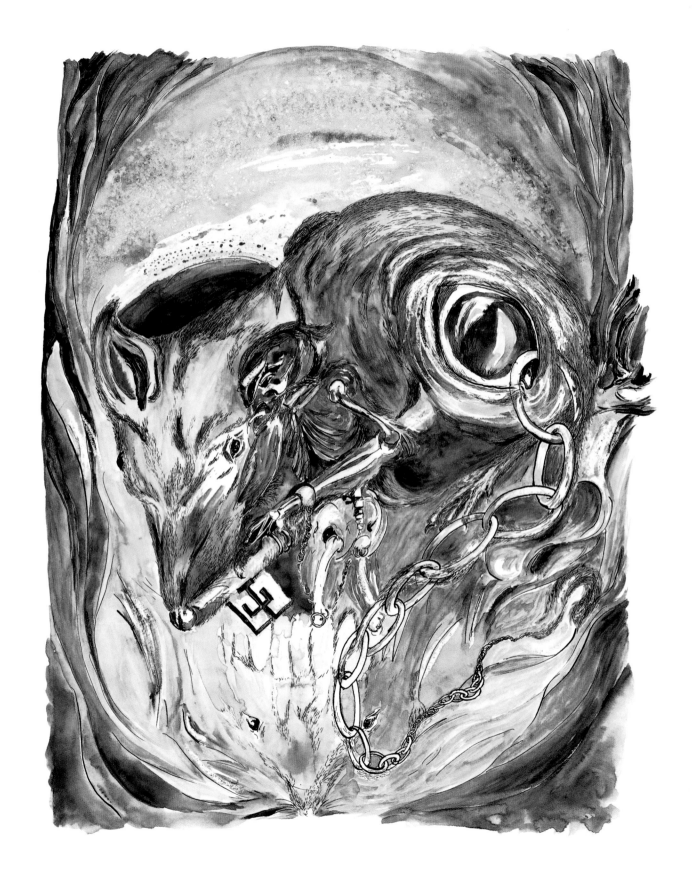

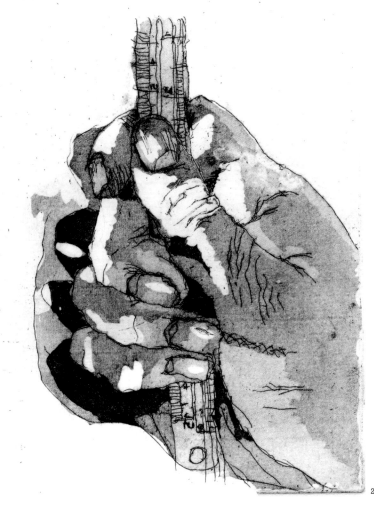

2

3

Katrina Hansford

1. Rats

College Southampton Solent University

Medium Watercolour, pen and ink

Brief One of a series of images produced to illustrate MR James' 'Selected Ghost Stories'.

Course Leader Derek Rodgers

Course BA(Hons) Illustration

Mary Pullen

2. La Main Gauche

College London College of Communication

Medium Etching and aquatint

Brief To produce an edition of 4 identical prints using the etching method. Student to decide on content of the image.

Course Leader Michael Brunwin

Phil Moss

3. Poor Knights Of St. Chad

College Stafford College

Medium Oil

Brief Create a mock book jacket cover image for a piece of historical fiction, without type. In this case, Bernard Cornwell's 'Lords of the North'.

Course Leader Iain Lowe

Course HND Graphics and Illustration

Ming Li

1. Blink

College Loughborough University

Medium Mixed media

Brief Blink is a book about the power of intuition. Produce a cover design that reflects the original open and intriguing quality of the book.

Course Leader Andrew Selby

Course BA Illustration

2. Help Yourself

College Loughborough University

Medium Digital

Brief Help Yourself is a teenager's self-help book. Being a teenager isn't easy in today's world but it brings with it massive opportunities and it's much more exciting than being an adult.

Course Leader Andrew Selby

Course BA Illustration

3. Write A Letter!

College Loughborough University

Medium Collage

Brief Produce an illustration that celebrates and encourages letter writing.

Course Leader Andrew Selby

Course BA Illustration

3

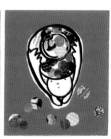

3

4

Ming Li

1. Shower With A Friend

College Loughborough University

Medium Mixed media

Brief A series of illustrations on how to be green.

Course Leader Andrew Selby

Course BA Illustration

2. Lost And Found

College Loughborough University

Medium Mixed media

Brief Illustrate the relationship between lost and found.

Course Leader Andrew Selby

Course BA Illustration

Phillip Evans

3. And They Swam And They Swam Right Over The Dam

College North Wales School of Art and Design

Medium Pen & ink and digital

Brief Inspired by the old children's song.

Course Leader Yadzia Williams

Course BA(Hons) Illustration

Katie Edwards

4. Annoyance

College Leeds Metropolitan University

Medium Lith photography and screenprinting

Brief From a series of 15 pieces exploring what hands symbolise and metaphors associated with hands.

Course Leader Mick Marsden

Course BA (Hons) Graphic Arts and Design

the zoo

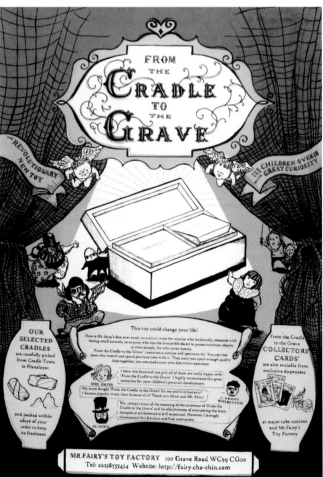

2

3

Rachel Tudor Best

1. Zoo

College Hereford College of the Arts

Medium Mixed media

Brief Design a poster to advertise
London Zoo.

Course Leader Mark Jackson

Course BA Illustration

Haruka Shinji

2. Journey

College Kingston University

Medium Pen and computer

Brief Drawing for business card.

Course Leader Geoff Grandfield

Course Illustration and Animation

3. From The Cradle To The
   Grave Poster

College Kingston University

Medium Screen print

Brief One of the drawings of a personal
project called "From the Cradle to the Grave".

Course Leader Geoff Grandfield

Course Illustration and Animation

Sam Griffiths

1. Your New God

College Stockport College of Further and Higher Education

Medium Mixed media

Brief Self initiated brief about the opposing theories of evolution and religion.

Course Leader Ian Parkin

Course BA Hons Graphic Design

2. Ancient Japan

College Stockport College of Further and Higher Education

Medium Mixed media

Brief Create an illustration as part of a poster campaign promoting Japan as a tourist destination.

Course Leader Ian Parkin

Course BA Hons Graphic Design

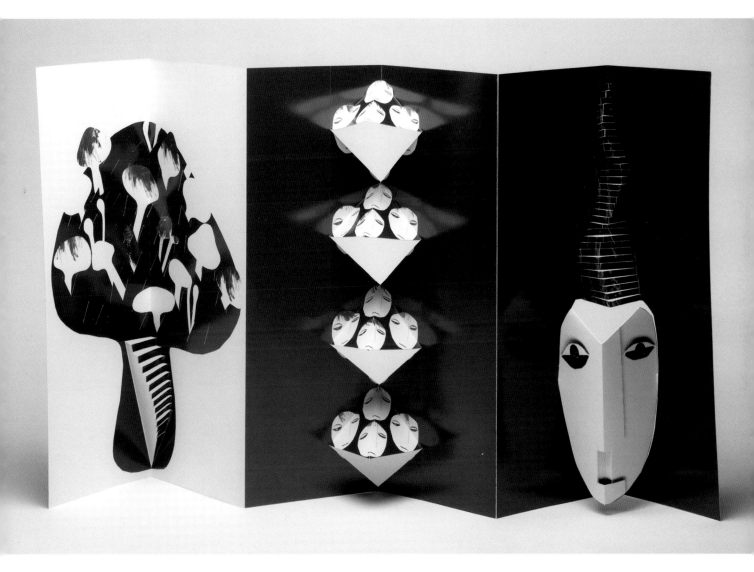

Jin Cho Youn

Kafka On The Shore

College London College of Communication
Medium Pop up book

brief This project is an illustration series for the
book 'Kafka on the shore' by Haruki Murakami.
The elements of realism and surrealism
captured my interest and gave me a challenge
to illustrate for this particular book.

Course leader Paul Bowman
Course title GMD / Illustration

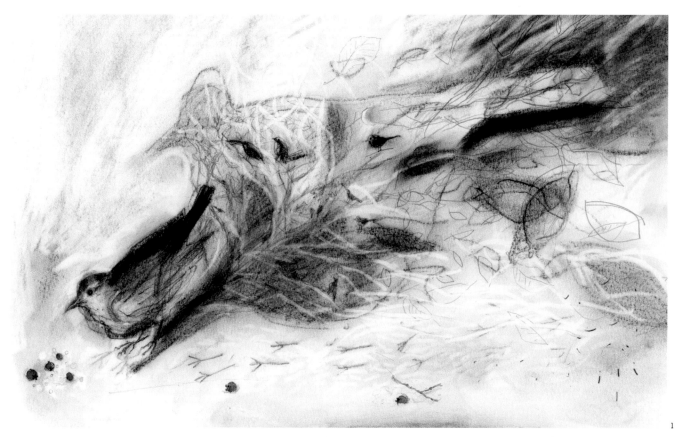

Alice Wood

1. When The Bird Died

College Cambridge School of Art

Medium Pencil and watercolour

Brief Write and illustrate a story book for children, about the journey of a nightingale's soul, looking for a new home.

Course Leader Martin Salisbury

Course MA Children's Book Illustration

2. They Told Stories

College Cambridge School of Art

Medium Watercolour

Brief Write and illustrate a book for children, about the journey of a nightingale's soul, looking for a new home.

Course Leader Martin Salisbury

Course MA Children's Book Illustration

3

Jordan Cross

3. Allergy To Modern Life

College University of Hertfordshire

Medium Hand drawn and Photoshop.

Brief Investigate all the things you dislike about modern life and create a finished response in whichever way you see fit.

Course Leader Paul Burgess

Course
BA Hons Graphic Design and Illustration

Anton Strickland Nelson

4. Swimming Pool

College Oxford and Cherwell Valley College

Medium Digital and mixed media

Brief Design an illustration to accompany a corporate editorial on Events Management.

Course Leader Neil Mabbs

Course BA Graphic Design and Illustration

4

Jenny Robins

Magpies

College Solent University

Medium Ink

Brief Endpaper for Magpies short stories book, also used in variously sized prints for self promotion.

Course Leader Derek Rogers

Course BA Illustration

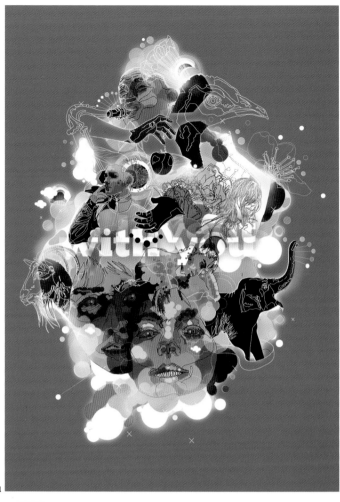

Brian Chia

1. I Love It With You

College Middlesex University

Medium Digital

Brief 'I love it with you' explores personal emotions and feelings encompassing his life.

Course Leader Gordon Davies

Course Media Art

2. Aesthetic Egoism

College Middlesex University

Medium Digital

Brief Aesthetic egoism explores the relationship between shapes, colours, lines and form.

Course Leader Gordon Davies

Course Media Art

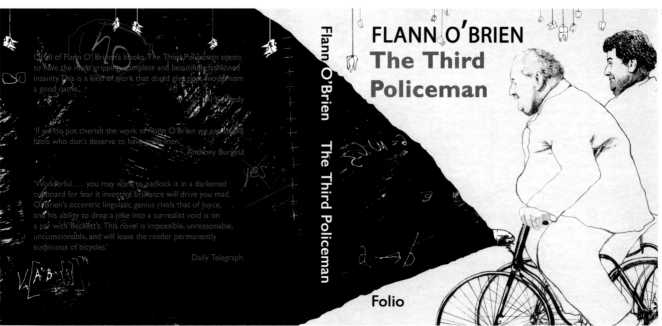

Fatime Sza'szi

1. Illustrated Quotes And Sayings Book

College University College Falmouth

Medium Mixed media (oil and Photoshop)

Brief To illustrate a quote by Willam Shakespeare: '"Thou know'st 'tis common; all that lives must die, passing through nature to eternity"'.

Course Leader Alan Male

Course Illustration (BA)

2. The Third Policeman

College University College Falmouth

Medium Mixed media (ink, watercolour and Photoshop)

Brief To create a book cover for Flann O'Brien's 'The Third Policeman'.

Course Leader Alan Male

Course Illustration (BA)

3

4

Amy Abbott

3. Wolf

College University of Leeds

Medium Pencil, ink, wax crayon

Brief Illustration based on the fairytale Red Riding Hood. The wolf's feelings towards Red Riding Hood are becoming more romantic.

Course Leader Kevin Laycock

Course
BA (Hons) Mixed Media Textile Design

Carys Williams

4. Pi

College University College Falmouth

Medium Acrylic on canvas

Brief Illustrating "Pi" a song taken from the Kate Bush album 'Aerial'. About a man obsessed with the calculation of Pi.

Course Leader Alan Male

Course BA(Hons) Illustration

Freddy Morris

1. Street Scene

College Middlesex University

Medium Etching

Brief Final major project, exploring etching with aquatint.

Course Leaders
Andrew Baker and Nancy Slonims

Course BA (Hons) Illustration

2. Tryptych

College Middlesex University

Medium Etching

Brief Final major project, exploring etching with aquatint.

Course Leaders
Andrew Baker and Nancy Slonims

Course BA (Hons) Illustration

3

4

Jessica Allan

3. Split In Two

College Middlesex University

Medium Pen collage and Photoshop

Brief Illustrate three bad things and three good things that happen to you over the summer holidays.

Course Leader Nancy Slonims

Gemma Watson

4. Urban Landscape

College York College

Medium Mixed media and digital

Brief Study the urban landscape and its relationship to you. Consider architecture, people, open space, movement and lighting.

Course Leader Ben Clowes

Course HNC Fine Arts

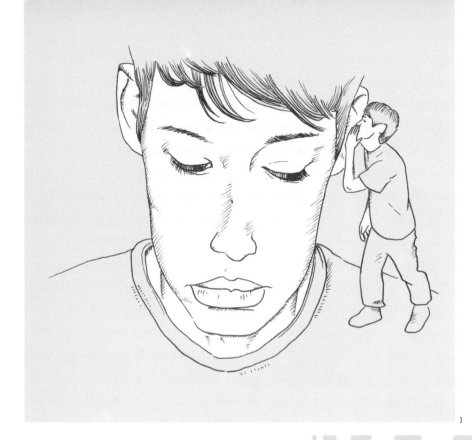

Jonathan Unwin

1. Whisper
....

College Havering College

Medium Pen and digital

Brief Imagination.

Course Leader Tony Branch

Course BA(Hons) Graphic Design

Michael Thorp

2. Cot
....

College Coventry University

Medium Acrylic on canvas

Brief Personal project to illustrate Ivor Cutler's poem 'Baby sits'.

Course Leader Glyn Brewerton

Course Fine Art and Illustration

1

2

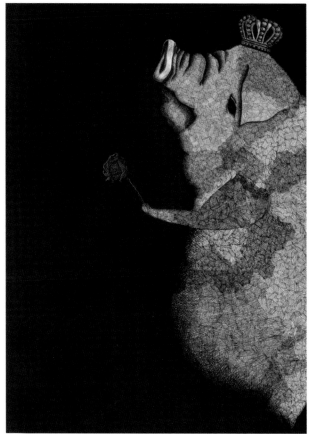

3

4

5

Nathan Sissons

3. Train Scene

College Middlesex Universsity

Medium Etching

Brief To illustrate 'The Plague' by Camus using etching.

Course Leaders
Andrew Baker and Nancy Slonims

Course BA(Hons) Illustration

4. Captive Scene

College Middlesex Universsity

Medium Etching

Brief To illustrate 'The Outsider' by Camus, using etching.

Course Leaders
Andrew Baker and Nancy Slonims

Course BA(Hons) Illustration

Shun Matsuzaka

5. The Enchanted Pig

College University College Falmouth

Medium Mixed Media

Brief Poster illustration for 'The Enchanted Pig' by Young Vic.

Course Leader Alan Male

Course BA (Hons) Illustration

1

2

3

4

5

Katie Simpson

1. Sister

College Kingston University

Medium Collage and acrylic

Brief 'Sister' is from a series of images about Venus and Serena Williams. It is about their sister who was killed in a drive by shooting.

Course Leader Geoff Grandfield

Course BA(Hons) Illustration and Animation

Samuel Bell

2. CTU

College The Arts Institute at Bournemouth

Medium Paper collage

Brief A fantastical depiction of an imaginary surveillance control centre for my final major project based around the theme of surveillance.

Course Leader Joel Lardner

Tracey Long

3. There Was An Old Lady Who Swallowed A Cow

College Herefordshire College of Art & Design

Medium Pencil, watercolour and collage

Brief To illustrate; There was an old lady who swallowed a fly. This image represents the swallowing of a cow!

Course Leader Mark Jackson

Course BA (Hons) Illustration

Alex Strang

4. Games As Children

College London College of Communication

Medium Pencil and pencil crayon

Brief Book illustration about the life of Ivor Cutler.

Course Leader Paul Bowman

Course GMD Illustration

Rosemary Squire

5. Gordon Brown's Record As Chancellor

College Loughborough University

Medium 3 Dimensional

Brief To create a personal interpretation of Gordon Brown in a satirical setting.

Course Leader Andrew Selby

Course BA(Hons) Illustration

"Maybe if I lost a few pounds, and did something with my hair, and had myself stretched, I could look perfect too. I turned around again. Or maybe not."

Best friends Gemma and Amy have no time for Miss Perfect Teenagers - tall, thin blondes whose only talk is of boys and fashion. At least they didn't. Now, all of a sudden, Amy's changed. She's into salads and diet Cokes, she's got a new hairstyle, wardrobe and set of friends. Gemma, meanwhile, finds herself part of a group of unglamorous oddballs named the Martians. Will she follow Amy or find her own way?

£5.99

11062003

Walker Books

Tall thin & blonde

Dyan Sheldon

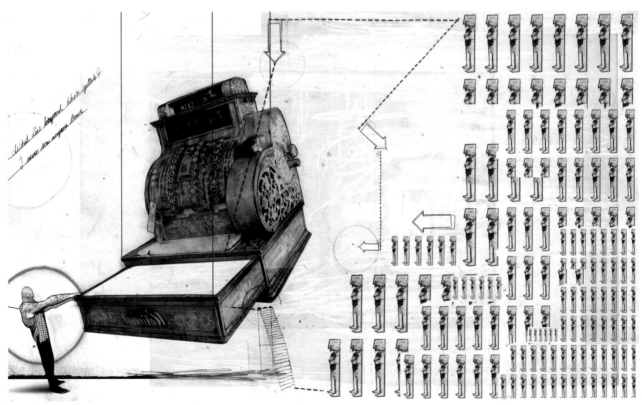

1

2

3

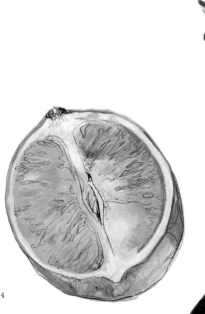

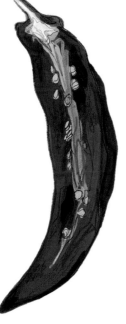

4

Amy Bannister

1. Tall, Thin & Blonde

College Cumbria Institute of the Arts

Medium Fabric and linear illustration

Brief To create teenage novel book cover illustrations for the D&AD brief set through Cumbria Institute of the Arts.

Course Leader Simon Davies

Course BA(Hons) Graphic Design

Daniel Boyle

2. The Till

College Kingston University

Medium Pencil and digital

Brief To explore and reinvent the mythical character of Charun the Ferryman.

Course Leader Geoff Grandfield

Course BA(Hons) Illustration and Animation

Emilia Robledo

3. The Sultan's Elephant

College
North Wales School of Art and Design

Medium Pencil, charcoal, ink and digital

Brief To create atmospheric and emotionally engaging illustrations for this moving tale by Royal de Luxe about a little girl lost in time.

Course Leader Sue Thornton

Course BA (Hons) Design: Illustration for Children's Publishing

Heather Rothwell

4. Rainbow Of Foods

College University College Falmouth

Medium Gouache and water colour pencils

Brief Illustration for the quotation "eating a rainbow of foods is seriously good for your health" cut to white + double page spread.

Course Leader Alan Male

Course BA (Hons) Illustration

4

Jisun Lee

1. The Tiny Room

College Brighton University

Medium Mixed media

Brief Narrative illustration for a picture book - a theme of fate and relationship between imagination and reality through the window.

Course Leaders George Hardie/Margaret Huber

Course Sequential Design/Illustration

Katy Louise Hudson

2. Untitled

College Bath Spa University

Medium Ink and acrylic paint

Brief CD booklet for the band "Wardrobe". Album title: "Behind Closed Doors".

Course Leaders Angela Hogg/Tim Vyner

Course BA Graphic Communication

Judith Knight

3. Balconies And Bedsteads

College Stockport College

Medium Digital and Mixed media

Brief To illustrate an Editorial based on an article reviewing 3 books on unusual stories in which people have decorated their homes and dolls houses.

Course Leader Ian Murray/Gary Spicer

Course BA(Hons) Illustration, Design and Visual Arts

Gemma Baxter

4. Cake

College Kingston University

Medium Mixed media

Brief Personal project, from a body of work based around the theme of cakes.

Course Leader Geoff Grandfield

Course BA Illustration and Animation

Alex Gardner

1. Noah's Ark

College Loughborough University

Medium Digital

Brief A development from the Dorling Kindersley brief 'Amazing Animals', using Noah's Ark to show how the animal world is inter-linked.

Course Leader Andrew Selby

Course BA(Hons) Illustration

Holly Jesty

2. A Snail Shell For Slugs

College University of Plymouth

Medium Collagraph print

Brief This was the design for an EP sleeve for a Plymouth based band, that was part of a self-negotiated project for university. I also produced designs for other promotional items such as posters and flyers.

Course Leaders
Ashley Potter, Jo Davies, Wendy Smith

Course BA(Hons) Design: Illustration

Thomas Evans

3. Window Scene

College Central Staint Martins

Medium Ink on paper

Course Leader Steve Roberts

Course Post Graduate: Animation

Rachel Boulton

4. Saeki's Day Out

College University College Falmouth

Medium Dip pen with inks

Brief A light hearted children's illustration following Saeki and Jeffery's journey of discovery. The method used was dip pen and inks to create a bright and appealing artwork, with much to look at, entertaining for parent and child.

Course BA(Hons) Illustration

When they got to the top of the hill Saeki and Jeffery the bear saw the beach and all the people swimming in the sea.

Chris Martin

1. Martinsville

College Southampton Solent University

Medium Pen, ink and Photoshop

Brief Open brief. To create an entirely imagined place, and visualise it in the way I saw most interesting.

Course Leader Derek Rogers

Course BA(Hons) Illustration

David Cole

2. Sophie Pitt-Turnbull Discovers America

College Middlesex Universsity

Medium Drawing and digital manipulation

Brief To illustrate the book by Dyan Sheldon.

Course Leaders
Andrew Baker and Nancy Slonims

Course BA(Hons) Illustration

3. I Conquer Britain

College Middlesex Universsity

Medium Drawing and digital manipulation

Brief To illustrate the book by Dyan Sheldon.

Course Leaders
Andrew Baker and Nancy Slonims

Course BA(Hons) Illustration

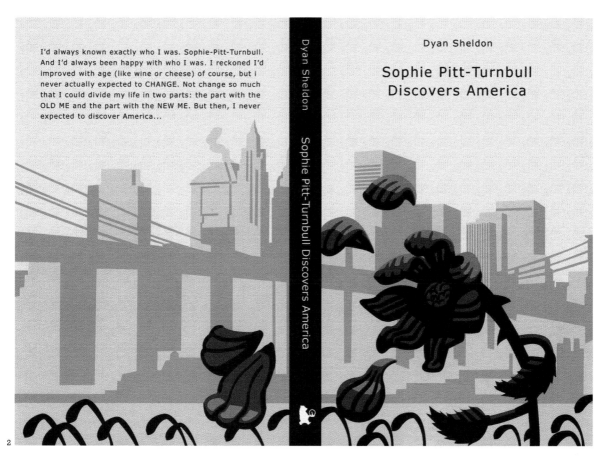

Dyan Sheldon

Sophie Pitt-Turnbull
Discovers America

I'd always known exactly who I was. Sophie-Pitt-Turnbull. And I'd always been happy with who I was. I reckoned I'd improved with age (like wine or cheese) of course, but i never actually expected to CHANGE. Not change so much that I could divide my life in two parts: the part with the OLD ME and the part with the NEW ME. But then, I never expected to discover America...

Dyan Sheldon

Sophie Pitt-Turnbull Discovers America

2

3

Dyan Sheldon

I Conquer Britain

I felt more like Alice in Wonderland than a visitor to a foreign country. Like I'd fallen down a rabbit hole and into a world where everything kind of looked the same but wasn't. They might all speak English in London, but that didn't mean I could understand them. It was really lucky that I liked a challenge.

Dyan Sheldon

I Conquer Britain

Index of illustrators

Index of illustrators

Alan Heighton 207

T 01302 743 927
M 07708 584 287
E alheighton@hotmail.com
W alanheighton.co.uk

Lewis Heriz 209

M 07841 342 738
E hello@lewisheriz.com
W lewisheriz.com

Tobias Hickey 203

T 01273 677 545
M 07791 558 262
E digitalsoup@talktalk.net
W tobiashickey.talktalk.net

John Holcroft 217

T 01709 892 726
E mail@johnholcroft.com
W johnholcroft.com

Peter Horridge 202

T 01829 261 801
M 07775 583 760
F 01829 261 802
E peter@horridge.com
W horridge.com
A Central Illustration Agency
T 020 7420 8925

Frazer Hudson 190-192

T 01142 682 861
M 07973 616 054
E frazer@hudsonfamily.demon.co.uk
W frazerhudson.com

Katy Louise Hudson 264

T 01642 282 080
M 07943 347 228
E katyhuds@hotmail.co.uk
W katyhudson.co.uk

David Humphries 116-117

T 020 8503 6012
M 07973 831 724
F 020 8503 6012
E david@davidhumphries.com
W davidhumphries.com

Rod Hunt 84-85

M 07931 588 750
E rod@rodhunt.com
W rodhunt.com

Philip Hurst 214

T 01303 872 581
E philip_hurst@hotmail.com
W philiphurst.com

Ruth Hydes 124

T 01270 841 836
M 07814 074 192
F 01270 841 836
E ruthhydes@btopenworld.com
W ruthhydes.co.uk

Marcus Irwin 131

T 01273 206 925
M 07875 004 341
E marcus@solskin.co.uk
W solskin.co.uk

Holly Jesty 266

M 07736 071 545
E holly.jesty@hotmail.co.uk
W myspace.com/hollyjestyillustrations

Adrian Johnson 12-13

T 020 7430 0722
M 07958 670 750
E info@adrianjohnson.co.uk
E adrian_johnson@mac.com
W adrianjohnson.co.uk
W blackconvoy.com
A Central Illustration Agency
T 020 7420 8925

Matthew Johnson 204

M 07775 902 507
E matthewjohnson@hotmail.com

Ben Jones 204

T 0161 368 7309
M 07958 438 735
E illustrationben@hotmail.co.uk
W giantillustration.com

Satoshi Kambayashi 110-111

T 01273 771 539
M 07739 179 107
F 01273 771 539
E satoshi.k@virgin.net
W satillus.com

Chris Kasch 201

T 020 8422 2416
E christopherkasch@aol.com
W chriskasch.co.uk
A Central Illustration Agency
T 020 7240 8925
W centralillustration.com

Alex Kemp 219

T 01702 354 045
M 07908 914 511
E kempsoulbrother@yahoo.co.uk
W kempart.co.uk

Steve King 207

T 0118 986 6961
M 07876 015 516
E skart@btinternet.com
W steveking-art.co.uk

Judith Knight 265

M 07941 798 052
E judithknight3@yahoo.co.uk
W judithknight.port5.com

Trevor Sylvester Lake MA 68-69

T 07916 260 505
E trevsdesign@yahoo.com
E trev@bluecherrycreative.com
W bluecherrycreative.com

Alexandra Lazar 206

T 020 8444 6394
M 07932 667 556
F 020 8444 6394
E info@cyanworks.com
W cyanworks.com

Jisun Lee 264

M 07766 088 638
E lee.jisun@gmail.com
W jisunlee.kr

Fritha Lewin 121

M 07736 947 267
E frithalewin@yahoo.co.uk
W fritha.org

Ming Li 242-244

M 07903 595 900
E ming.c.li@gmail.com
W my.studio.org.uk/littleming

Henning Löhlein 214

T 0117 929 9077
M 07711 285 202
F 0117 929 9077
E henning@lohlein.com
W lohlein.com

Tracey Long 260

T 01989 762 083
M 07765 946 822
E traceyalong@aol.com

David Lyttleton 149

T 01782 613 564
M 07958 421 092
E david.lyttleton@virgin.net

Peter Mac 172

T 01273 706 914
M 07734 593 448
E peter@brighton.co.uk
W peter-mac.com

Andrew MacGregor 197

T 020 7837 4070
M 07880 556 646
E ask@andymacgreor.com
W andymacgregor.com
A Début Art
T 020 7636 1064
E info@debutart.com
W debutart.com

Clare Mallison 212

M 07947 306 541
E mail@claremallison.com
W claremallison.com
A Anna Goodson Management
T 514 482 0488

Naomi Manning 216

M 07903 478 957
E info@naomillustration.co.uk
W naomillustration.co.uk

Tim Marrs 201

T 020 8653 8044
M 07714 062 447
E tim@timmarrs.co.uk
W timmarrs.co.uk
A Central Illustration Agency
T 020 7836 1106/020 7240 8925

Chris Martin 268

T 020 8889 5147
M 07984 621 666
E chris@mrchrismartin.co.uk
W mrchrismartin.co.uk

Steve May 198

M 07790 033 786
A Arena
T 0845 050 7600
E info@arenaworks.com
W arenaworks.com

Shun Matsuzaka 259

M 07957 195 057
E unko102@hotmail.com
W illustrashun.com

David McConochie 126

T 01915 100 702
M 07970 613 130
E davidmcconochie@hotmail.com
W davidmcconochie.co.uk
A The Art Market
T 020 7407 8111
W artmarketillustration.com

Adrian B McMurchie 120

T 0141 564 8004
M 07901 767 393
F 0141 564 8004
E adrian@amcmurchie.com
W amcmurchie.com

Index of illustrators

T Telephone **M** Mobile **F** Fax **E** Email **W** Web **A** Agent

Index of illustrators

AOI **Resources**

PUBLICATIONS

SURVIVE
The Illustrator's Guide to a Professional Career
Published by the AOI and last revised in 2001, Survive is the only comprehensive and in-depth guide to illustration as a professional career. Established illustrators, agents, clients and a range of other professionals have contributed to this fourth edition. Each area of the profession, including portfolio presentation, self-promotion and copyright issues are looked at in detail. The wealth of information in Survive makes it absolutely indispensable to the newcomer and also has much to offer the more experienced illustrator.

THE ILLUSTRATOR'S GUIDE TO LAW AND BUSINESS PRACTICE
Updated, expanded and redesigned with contemporary illustrations this comprehensive guide covers all aspects of the law likely to affect illustrators. It contains recommended terms and conditions, advice on calculating fees, how to write a licence agreement and protect yourself against exploitative practices.

The handbook has been written by Simon Stern, a renowned expert on illustration and the law, and is the result of many years of research. It has been approved by intellectual property experts, law firm Finers Stephens Innocent. The Illustrator's Guide to Law and Business Practice replaces the now discontinued publication Rights – the illustrator's guide to professional practice.

REPORT ON ILLUSTRATION FEES AND STANDARDS OF PRICING
In 2005, the AOI have first published a report entitled 'Illustration Fees and Standards of Pricing'. The publication was updated in April 2007 with newest information from an online survey, new AOI data from the last two years and invaluable contributions from agents, art buyers and selected working professionals.

Properly researched costing and pricing structures are a central plank in maintaining business viability. Illustrators should consider the true cost of their services when determining rates. AOI hopes that this report will encourage both illustrators and commissioners to be aware of the importance of carefully considered pricing.

CLIENT DIRECTORIES
The Publishing Directory lists ca. 180 and the Editorial Directory more than 300 illustration clients with full contact details; the Advertising Directory holds details of over 200 advertising agencies who commission illustration – providing an invaluable source of information for all practitioners. Each directory includes notes of what kind of illustration is published by the client and we update and add contact details to each list every year.

VAROOM
the journal of illustration and made images
Varoom is a magazine devoted to exploring the world of illustration and image-making. It looks at practitioners from around the world who are making significant contributions to the art of illustration, and provides writers, commentators and illustrators with a platform from which to take a critical look at trends and developments in the illustrated image.

Published three times a year. 90 pages, ISSN 1750-483X, available in specialist bookshops in the UK, Europe, USA and Canada, free to members.

www.varoom-mag.com

To order publications online visit the AOI's online shop on www.theaoi.com

To subscribe to Varoom go to www.varoom-mag.com

For further information please contact the Association of Illustrators on +44 (0)20 7613 4328 or email info@theaoi.com

INFORMATION

UP POSTER
Published quarterly, UP is a collectible item each time featuring another unique image-maker. UP not only looks good on your wall it also keeps you up to date with AOI news and events, reports on important industry developments and recommends exhibitions that could inspire you. UP is designed by award winning design duo Non-Format, who also created the eye-catching look of Varoom.

DESPATCH Newsletter
Now published monthly, Despatch brings you the latest industry news, AOI events information, campaigns, initiatives and reviews of relevant exhibitions and publications. To subscribe, visit www.theaoi.com/submissions

www.THEAOI.com
illustration resources for commissioners and practitioners
Visit the AOI's website for details of the Association's activities, including the current Despatch newsletter, and articles from our previous membership magazine, The Journal, details of forthcoming events and campaigns, the AOI's history, and to order publications, book tickets and browse online portfolios.

The AOI would like to **thank**

… all members of the jury for applying their expertise to the difficult task of selecting the best of all entries now published in this book. As usual, special thanks go to **Simon Sharville** for his creative impact and diplomacy during the design process and **Sabine Reimer** for her usual efficiency and cheerful dedication during the production of Images 32.

We are also very grateful to **Jill Calder** who gave us her illustration **'Tulips'** to create an eye-catching cover and **Kenneth Andersson**, whose image **'Big Dog'** we used for the promotion of the Call for Entry for Images 33.

Images 32 could not have been organised without the help of our dedicated casual staff and volunteers and we are very grateful for their invaluable assistance: **Martha Lineham and Zoe Connors**.

Last but not least, we are grateful for the support of the many organisations and individuals who contribute to the success of the Images exhibition and annual by submitting their work for others to judge.

The AOI Council and staff

arena

THE ARTWORKS

début **art**

theguardian

PRIVATE VIEW

SEVENTH ISSUE OUT AUGUST 08

www.varoom-mag.com

Illustration by Jonny Voss